GO FORTH
IN PEACE

GO FORTH IN PEACE

Orthodox Perspectives on Mission

Compiled and edited
by Ion Bria

World Council of Churches, Geneva

ISBN 2–8254–0861–1

© 1986 World Council of Churches, 150 route de Ferney,
1211 Geneva 20, Switzerland

WCC Mission Series No. 7

Phototypeset by Input Typesetting Ltd., London

Printed in Switzerland

TABLE OF CONTENTS

Foreword vii

PART I

1. The theological foundations for mission 3
2. The church and mission 10
3. Liturgy and mission... 17
4. Holy scripture, proclamation and liturgy 24
5. The good news and evangelistic witness 30
6. Mission as "Liturgy after the liturgy" 38
7. Witness and service... 47
8. Monastic life and renewal in mission 52
9. Mission to all peoples....................................... 56
10. History of Orthodox missions 64
11. The unity of the church and the unity of churches.. 69

PART II

1. Ecumenical convictions on mission and evangelism   75
2. The eucharist: bread and wine for pilgrims on
   their apostolic journey...................................... 92
3. Christian witness – common witness.................... 95

Consultations.. 101

FOREWORD

This is the revised edition of the book with the same title published by the Commission on World Mission and Evangelism (offset print) in 1982. The first edition, consisting of a selected body of material from several Orthodox consultations on mission organized by the CWME (1973-1980), was translated into several languages and widely distributed in many countries. The present text includes new chapters on the contextualization of mission and the history of Orthodox mission from recent Orthodox conferences and meetings (see list of consultations, page 101), as well as Orthodox contributions to the ecumenical convergences on mission, evangelization and common Christian witness as formulated in present documents of the WCC.

This edition has an anniversary character since it is published on the occasion of the commemoration of the 1100 years since the death of St Methodius (885), who together with his brother Cyril was sent from Thessaloniki, Greece, to preach the gospel in the slavic languages to the peoples in Central Europe.

This book is intended to be a guidebook for the use of parish priests, theological students, catechists, preachers and faithful called to the ministry of the proclamation of the good news. It is hoped that this "going forth in peace" provokes and stimulates the missionary spirit within Orthodoxy today. It shows that the potential of the Orthodox in the area of mission and evangelism is vast and needs special cultivation. It also shows that the Orthodox have a rich tradition of witness which they bring to the *oikoumene*, to the universal church.

A theological analysis and missiological evaluation of the present body of material will be the subject of a future publication in the WCC mission series.

Ion Bria
Secretary for Orthodox Studies
and Relationships, CWME

Part I

1. THE THEOLOGICAL FOUNDATIONS FOR MISSION

The Importance of Trinitarian Theology

The mission of the church is based on Christ's mission. A proper understanding of this mission requires, in the first place, an application of trinitarian theology. Christ's sending of the apostles is rooted in the fact that Christ himself is sent by the Father in the Holy Spirit (John 20:21-33). The significance of this scriptural assertion for the concept of mission is commonly recognized, but the trinitarian theology, which is implied in it, deserves more attention than it normally receives.

Trinitarian theology points to the fact that God is in God's own self a life of communion and that God's involvement in history aims at drawing humanity and creation in general into this communion with God's very life. The implications of this assertion for understanding mission are very important: mission does not aim primarily at the propagation or transmission of intellectual convictions, doctrines, moral commands, etc., but at the transmission of the life of communion that exists in God. The "sending" of mission is essentially the sending of the Spirit (John 14:26), who manifests precisely the life of God as communion (I Cor. 13:13).

The salvation of the world should be seen as a "programme" of the holy trinity for the whole of creation. The kingdom of God is the inner movement and the final goal not only of every human adventure, but of all the dynamic of the universe. True life is life in the holy trinity, in Christ by the Spirit coming from and oriented towards the Father.

The Centrality of Christ

In our faith, Christ occupies the central place in the act of confessing, for he is the dynamic factor in Christian confession in the world. Following the biblical and kerygmatic tradition of the church, we confess the incarnation of the Logos of God the Father, the mediator through the work of the Paraclete – for our regeneration and the restoration of our communion with God – in the divine-human person of Christ. Thus the Logos of God is not only saviour but also creator. He is our *centre* in a double sense: as divine Logos, source and model of our reason, and as initiating partner of our dialogue with him. As the divine-human hypostasis, the centre of everybody and everything, he is the *partner* and the creative and generative *source* of the dialogue with him and among human beings. He is the Logos of all things and the Logos is the image of the Father. The world has an ontological basis in God, because all things are linked to the Logos. They represent the diversification of the reason of the Logos. At the same time their link and their unity in a harmonious whole are grounded in the non-differentiated unity of the personal Logos. While things are material, tangible and intelligible images of the diversified reasons and thoughts of the Logos, the human being is the image of the Logos himself as a person who thinks.

The Son of God has assumed the fullness of our humanity into himself; in that process, he affirms, he heals and restores humanity by placing it in himself, and therefore in the holy trinity. It is the great mystery of the perfect divine-human unity that becomes the source-spring of the new life of the world. In making Christ central in our theological under-standing, however, the trinitarian and incarnational aspects of the new life should always be held together, in a christo-centric but not in a christomonistic manner.

The Incarnation
In order to establish the communion between God 'and humanity, broken because of the fall in its cosmic dimension, the Logos, in his capacity as a person, has introduced himself more intimately into creation and into human history. He is incarnate through the Holy Spirit. Through his incarnation he has revealed the meaning of things. He has restored the bond with us and has renewed the human being. In Christ we find not only reason as the source of our common human reason, but *our total being* is lifted up to the image of God through participation in the Spirit. Through the same act the Logos has established a new relationship between the creator and the human being, an ontological relationship, dynamic not static, which is created and perfected through the ener-gies of God, effected by the Holy Spirit. By restoring us to our function the incarnate Logos communicates to us the power to liberate ourselves from our egotism, in order to

understand others and to enter into communion with them and with him. This is the interpersonal function of the Logos. Christ is thus the human being par excellence, the centre of creation, the central human who relates to all. He calls us to make humanity understand that it should not be content with its insufficient rationality and to help people to find the personal origin of reason that is to be found precisely in Christ.

In spite of the humanization of the Logos, we are still free to refuse communion with God. Hence also the presence of sin and evil, which have a real existence and which are opposed to the regenerative work of the Logos. Evil is at the root of the divisions and the passions that have separated us. But the incarnate Logos who effectively unites us establishes in the Holy Spirit the communion in the church that is the body of Christ. The church realizes the unifying message of the divine Logos, for the Logos is its centre and therefore the unifying basis for all humanity.

The Cross
Christ is sent into the world not as teacher, example, etc., but as a bearer of this divine life that aims at drawing the world into the way of existence that is to be found in the trinity. The understanding of Christ as the Logos of God in the early church served at that time to illustrate two things that are significant for mission. On the one hand it meant that Christ as the Logos, eternally existing in God as one of the trinity, is sent to the world as a bearer of the trinitarian life and not as a separate individual. On the other hand, it meant that as the cosmic Logos, the power that sustains the world, Christ was sent for no lesser purpose than to bring the world into the life of God. Christ's mission is, therefore, essentially the self-giving of the trinity so that the world may become a participant in the divine life.

This mission of Christ takes place in a "fallen" world and is met by the resistance of the "powers and principalities" of evil and sin. This has made the cross the inevitable passage of Christ's mission. Mission, therefore, takes place in the context of struggle and implies a conversion, a paschal and baptismal passage of the world into a "new creation." This is not a fight that manifests itself simply in the souls of individuals; it permeates all of social life through injustice, oppression, etc., and even the whole of natural existence through sickness and death.

The Resurrection

While the reality of the cross represents the inevitable context of mission as a clash between the trinitarian way of existence and the "powers and principalities" of sin, the resurrection of Christ throws light on mission in two fundamental ways. In the first place it points to the fact that the outcome of mission is beyond any doubt the defeat of the powers of sin in both its social and natural implications (the overcoming of death). Christ's ascension and constant intercession at the right hand of God sustain this assurance. Equally, however, the resurrection points to the fact that this outcome of mission is not controlled by historical forces but is eschatological in nature. It is the Spirit of God that raised Christ from the dead (Rom. 8:11). The church's mission cannot build up or bring about the kingdom. It can only announce its coming through the kerygma of the resurrection and point to it in a sacramental way.

Everything will be fully revealed and realized in the eschaton; meanwhile the church already participates in it through the first-fruits of the Holy Spirit. Therefore, it confesses this eschaton to be open, through the Logos, in the first-fruits of the Spirit, which are the source and power for advancing the whole of humanity towards the coming kingdom, and for giving to the world a joyful hope of the authentic and eternal life that follows the sacrifice of the cross.

It is important not only to keep the cross and resurrection together, but to keep the whole incarnate life of Christ as a single unit. There can be no Christian "theology of the cross" divorced from the annunciation to the Blessed Virgin, the birth, the baptism, and the public ministry ending in the resurrection, ascension, pentecost and second coming. It would be equally misleading to contrast a "theology of glory" and a "theology of the cross." The cross is where Christ was glorified ("Now is the Son of Man glorified," John 13:31). The glory of Christ was manifested also in the washing of the disciples' feet as in the cross and resurrection and in all the acts of the economy of salvation.

The Work of the Holy Spirit

Christians are often tempted to confine the activity of God the Holy Spirit to the church, or to individual human hearts or to the inspiration and illumination of the Bible.

But the Spirit was with Christ from the beginning of

creation, brooding upon it, giving life to it, bringing form and perfection to all things. Long before human beings appeared on the face of the earth, the Spirit has been at work in the world, proceeding eternally from the Father.

The church glorifies the Holy Spirit along with the Father and the Son, for the Spirit is creator, life-giver and perfector. He is with Christ always. It was the Spirit of the Lord who abode upon Jesus at baptism, and who anointed him to preach the good news (Luke 4:18-19). It is the Spirit who gives life (John 6:63), because it is the Spirit of him who raised Jesus from the dead (Rom. 8:11). To set the mind on the Spirit is life and peace (Rom. 8:6).

It is important to affirm these three elements about the work of the Spirit:

a) The whole saving activity of Christ is inseparable from the work of the Holy Spirit, and the christological and pneumatological affirmations should be kept integrally related to each other in a fully trinitarian context.

b) The work of the Holy Spirit as life-giver and perfector should be seen in its wider cosmic sense and not just in a narrow ecclesiastical or individual sense. It is the Spirit who makes *all* things new – the Spirit of the new creation.

c) The bread of life, the body and blood of our Lord, becomes that by the invocation of the Holy Spirit. The Holy Spirit is not an impersonal force, but the living Spirit of God, who is also the Spirit of the community, the Spirit who perfects and completes all the sacramental mysteries of the church.

Synergia
This is the deep foundation for the patristic teaching on salvation. It is not the case that we are equal partners with God or that God cannot act independently of us. *Synergia* means that God has chosen to work through us. God calls us to surrender ourselves to Christ in order that God may unite us to God's self and work through us, enhancing our freedom and in no way abolishing our personal subjectivity.

Our flesh is weak, but we are not daunted by the weakness of the flesh, for the word of God has become flesh. The life of Jesus Christ includes our bodies of flesh, our minds and wills and all our human faculties.

It is precisely in our weakness that the strength of God is manifested. The Spirit helps us in our weakness. When we acknowledge our natural limitations in humility and repentance, then God takes us and does his mighty acts through us. Where there is faith, God works through the feeble and the powerless. The apostles were not chosen because they were wise or learned, wealthy or powerful. The people of Israel were chosen when they were an enslaved people in Egypt. Not many of us Christians were chosen because we were wise and strong.

But weakness remains weakness where there is no repentance or faith. Our problem today is that we are so preoccupied with our past failures and present powerlessness that we do not set our minds on the Spirit of God, who is wise and powerful. So long as we put our trust in our own wisdom and resources, the Spirit of God does not do his mighty acts through us. "We have this treasure in earthen vessels, to show that the transcendent power belongs to God and not to us" (II Cor. 4:7). That transcendent power is not limited by our limitations, but only waits for our repentance and faith to receive that power.

The Call to Repentance and to Obedience to the Will of God
It is obvious that throughout history Christians have failed to be faithful and have obstructed the work of God in the world. God in Christ has equipped the church with all the gifts of the Spirit necessary for its upbuilding and its ministry; the eucharist and the other sacramental mysteries of the church as well as the provision of bishops, presbyters, and deacons, are all for this purpose. The fasts and feasts, the liturgical calendar and offices, the churches (parishes) and monasteries, the various ways of sanctifying different times and places, the growth of saints in the church, all these exist both for the healing of Christians, and for the mediation of the new life to the world. A rich tradition of iconography makes the unseen world of the holy events and persons physically present in the church.

In the church, the Spirit of God is at work despite our failures as Christians. Those who have the Spirit can discern the work of the Spirit in the church and in the world, despite human unbelief and disobedience. The Spirit has not abandoned the church or the world. Along with our confession of faith in God the Holy Spirit, we confess our belief also in the one, holy, catholic and apostolic church.

Yes, despite our failures – and they are many – God is at work. But that is no ground for complacency. Neither does that fact justify our failures. Our lack of love, however, hinders the Spirit. Our indiscipline makes the heart of God grieve. Because of our unbelief God does not do his great work of healing the sick, cleansing the leper, opening the eyes of the blind, as Christ did where there was faith.

So, the first step in effectively mediating the life of Christ to the world is to call ourselves to repentance and to a life of renewed faith and disciplined obedience to the will of God. The healing of nations demands that Christians be disciplined healers. We have to put to death the old Adam in us, and be clothed with the new man in Christ. The deep spiritual *askesis*, or discipline, of daily dying to ourselves and being born anew in Christ by the Spirit, has to be practised by all Christians, whether living in a monastery or not. *Theosis* is a continuing state of adoration, prayer, thanksgiving, worship, and intercession, as well as meditation and contemplation of the triune God and God's infinite love. This life of participation in the life and worship of the church and the "inner liturgy of the heart" constitute a foretaste of *theosis*, for all Christians, as they walk their pilgrim way through life. "Be still and know that I am God," says the Lord. We need to practise that deep silence of the Spirit, in order to receive the life of God and to mediate it to the world. We need also to "put on the whole armour of God, for our struggle is not against flesh and blood, but against the powers of darkness, against the spiritual hosts of evil" (Eph. 6:10-16).

2. CHURCH AND MISSION

It is in the fulfilment of our Lord's mandate to "Go and make disciples of all nations" (Matt. 28:16-20) that we find an authentic understanding of the church. The meaning of the Greek word for church, ecclesia (from 'εκ-καλῶ'), is to call out, to gather the people of God as a sign and manifestation of the kingdom of God.

Through the individual members of the body of Christ, the church is unequivocally committed to communicating the good *news* and to striving towards the growth, sanctification and wellbeing of this one body. Since the pentecost event, when the first disciples were filled with God's Holy Spirit, this communication was no longer an option but rather an obligation, a necessity: "For I am compelled to preach. Woe to me if I do not preach the gospel!" (I Cor. 9:16).

Thus, by definition, the church can never remain static nor satisfied with a status quo. It must continually be in mission, proclaiming, announcing and teaching the good news to the oikoumene, the whole inhabited earth: "You will receive power when the Holy Spirit comes on you, and you will be my witnesses in Jerusalem, and in all Judea and Samaria, and to the ends of the earth" (Acts 1:8).

The gospel, in order to be good news, must be communicated. All the people of God, together and individually, bear the responsibility for witnessing to the good news and for maintaining and preserving the catholicity of God's revelation to his people in every local church.

The Apostolicity of the Church

The kingdom of God which has come and is coming is presented to the world by the community of repentant and pardoned sinners, which is the body of Christ, the church. Despite the sins of its members and because the word lives in it, the church proclaims the kingdom of God to the world. Because the church is given the presence of the Holy Spirit as guarantee, the kingdom is in our midst, the end – the eschaton – is already accessible to the world. The kingdom is already at work in the world, a joyful hope. Therefore the church is an eschatological community, a pilgrim people, which lives in the ardent expectation of the return of its Lord and bears witness to him before the world.

Mission means the proclamation of the good news, i.e. of the coming of the kingdom: "The time is fulfilled, the kingdom of God is at hand; repent and believe in the gospel" (Mark 1:15). But Jesus only proclaims this good news to the "lost sheep of the house of Israel" (Matt. 15:24). Not until after his resurrection did he send his disciples beyond the frontiers of Israel: "Go forth, therefore, and make all nations my disciples; baptize men everywhere in the name of the Father and the Son and the Holy Spirit" (Matt. 28:19). But he commands them to wait in Jerusalem until he sends upon them the "Father's promised gift" and they are "clothed with power from on high" (Luke 24:29), and then he sends them "to be witnesses . . . to the end of the earth" (Acts 1:8).

The church thus discovers the splendour of the kingdom of God in the person of the risen Christ, revealed to the disciples of all times by the coming of the Holy Spirit, and in this way it finds the power to proclaim the kingdom to the ends of the earth. Rejoicing, therefore, in the communion of the Holy Spirit and marvelling at the resurrection, the church proclaims to the world the reign of "Jesus Christ crucified" (I Cor. 2:2), the reign of "Him who is and who was and who is to come" (Rev. 1:4; 1:8; 4:8).

Mission as Part of the Nature of the Church
The proclamation of the kingdom of God lies at the very heart of the church's vocation in the world. Mission belongs to the very nature of the church, whatever the conditions of its life, for without mission there is no church, because the church continues the work of humankind's salvation revealed and achieved by Jesus Christ our saviour. Only by the pentecostal outpouring of the Holy Spirit is the mission of the church possible and the apostolic community endowed with the power of the Spirit for the announcement of the gospel of the Christ who died and rose again for our salvation. The coming of the Holy Spirit in the church is not an isolated historic event in the past but a permanent gift which gives life to the church, ensuring its existence in the history of humanity, making possible its witness to the inaugurated kingdom of God. The Holy Spirit is the divine power

whereby the church is able to obey the command of the risen Lord: "Go forth to every part of the world and proclaim the good news to the whole creation" (Mark 16:15; cf. Luke 24:47 and Acts 1:8). This permanent pentecostal outpouring of the Spirit on the church is a reality in the church's worship, in its public prayer, in the Sunday celebration of the eucharist, but it overflows the limits of ecclesial worship and constitutes the inner dynamic that gives character to all expressions of and all activities in the life of the church.

Mission is not related exclusively to the "apostolicity," but to all the *notae* of the church, including unity, holiness and catholicity. This affects the concept of mission in a decisive way, since it removes it from the realm of quantity to become a qualitative reality; it is not the number of "converts" or the statistical membership of the church that can point to the existence of mission; the holiness, unity and catholicity (which is not to be confused with geographical expansion and universality) determine the notion of mission more than any success in numbers (Matt. 18:20).

The Eucharistic Community
The goal and aim of the proclamation of the gospel, and thus of mission, is the establishment of eucharistic communities in every locality, within its own context and culture and in its own language. These eucharistic communities, centred around worship and the celebration of the holy eucharist, will initiate the kingdom of God and become the focal point for active and concrete Christian witness, for mutual spiritual and material support and for teaching the members "to observe all that I have commanded you."

The local church, both clergy and laity in possession of the fulness of catholicity, must respond in obedience to the gospel and to the specific needs of its own situation and circumstances. The eucharistic community will witness most effectively through its own example of openness and unity, as well as through the spirituality and holiness of its individual members. These will be communicated through their active participation in the sacramental life of the community and through concrete expressions of love and concern for one another and for the whole body of Christ, in accordance with the teachings of our Lord in his parable of the last judgement (Matt. 25:36-41).

Challenges to the Missionary Calling of the Church

Within

Mission suffers and is seriously distorted or disappears whenever it is not possible to point to a community in history that reflects this trinitarian existence of communion. This happens whenever the church is so distorted or divided that it is no longer possible to recognize it as such a communion, or whenever mission is exercised without reference to the church, but with reference simply to the individuals or the social realities of history. Ecclesiological heresy, therefore, renders mission impossible or distorted.

Without

The church in our time should resist the temptation to insure itself, or even to enter into partnership with the authorities and powers of this world, lest it betray the most precious gift of the Spirit, namely, the liberty of the children of God. In all the struggles and conflicts that rend asunder the human family, the church should seek to reflect the sufferings, injustices and forms of violence (open or concealed), and to reverberate the cries and appeals of all those – Christians and non-Christians – who are persecuted for their faith and brutally treated in violation of human dignity and the basic principles of justice.

While weaknesses and betrayals of which the members of the church are guilty may all too easily obscure the witness, they cannot cancel out the fundamental calling of the church: "Heaven and earth will pass away, but my words will not pass away" (Matt. 24:35). This summons remains even if some of us are deaf to it; the power of death, the gates of Hades will not prevail against the church (cf. Matt. 16:18).

The People of God in Mission

It is the privilege of all the members of the eucharistic communities, clergy and laity, young and old, women and men, to participate in the ongoing mission of God. By virtue of their baptism, charismation and reception of the new life of the gospel as experienced in prayer, worship and communion, all have an apostolic calling to witness through the quality of their lives to the experience of the risen Christ. The emphasis, therefore, lies on the realization of the vocation of the whole people of God to live as a corporate witnessing community.

13

In order to understand Orthodoxy, we must remember that all believers are consecrated so as to live the good news inside as well as outside the temple of God: "The priesthood of believers is no longer limited to places of worship, to liturgical time and space. It is rather an immersion into the life of the human community through an evangelical witness" (*The Future of Orthodox Witness*). The believers enjoy the wondrous freedom of proclaiming the good news and witnessing to the Lord in a variety of ways best suited to the circumstances and the particular needs of the society in which they live.

Therefore, all categories of the people of God must be enabled to fulfil their potentials, exercise their manifold gifts and be involved in mission, as St Paul says in I Corinthians 12:27-31.

The Involvement of Women
Each member of the body of Christ must take on a full share of the mission of the church. To more effectively meet the needs of the church and its work in society, use must be made of the different charismata and contributions of both men and women.

Theological schools and church leadership are encouraged to examine at all levels the possibilities for new vocations for theologically trained women who can serve the emerging needs of the church.

Special courses also need to be given so as to make the training of women for church service more relevant and meaningful. These courses would also be open to women who seek to be better trained as laypersons capable of participating in the local, regional or national policy-making bodies of the church. Particular attention should be given to the vocation of the wives of priests.

Women who are called to full-time ministry in the church may consider a ministry in the sphere of the diaconate, remembering that in the early centuries of the church the deaconess played a significant role in fulfilling the true diakonia of the church. The role of the deaconesses in the Coptic Orthodox Church of Egypt and the Armenian Church in Constantinople could serve as an example for other Orthodox churches. The mother of God is the permanent point of reference for the mission of women in the Orthodox Church.

Youth and Mission

The revival of interest in mission and of missionary work within the Orthodox Church in recent years has been the result of the vision and efforts of Orthodox youth movements, notably through the Porefthendes, an Inter-Orthodox Missionary Centre related to Syndesmos, the fellowship of Orthodox youth organizations.

Today we must encourage this prophetic and apostolic role of youth by stimulating their full participation in the church and in missionary activities. Orthodox youth, whether in local or international movements, should be called upon to bring their fresh enthusiasm, vigour and new perspectives to Orthodox missionary efforts. Moreover, special attention should be given to the educating of young persons for mission.

Common Christian Witness

We are constantly confronted by situations in the secular society that require common Christian witness. Many of the Christian values are under attack. Only if we confront together the sinister influences of secularism will we be successful in asserting the way of life we believe to be essential for the wellbeing of the people of God.

On issues such as the sanctity of marriage, the stability of the family, human rights, abortion, peace, nuclear disarmament, etc., which affect all of us and not simply the Orthodox, we must speak and act together.

Other issues, such as the increase of migrant workers in certain areas of the world and the mobility of people as tourists, students and political refugees, call for common witness and solutions.

Our Orthodox churches and our people should be encouraged whenever possible to take part in and even initiate such a common witness. Two recent ecumenical texts may be of assistance in guiding our efforts: *Common Witness* and *Mission and Evangelism – An Ecumenical Affirmation.**

Principles of Mission

Inspired by the Holy Spirit, several principles have been followed in the church's witness from the very inception of the Christian church on the day of pentecost.

---

* Published by the Commisson on World Mission and Evangelism of the World Council of Churches, Geneva, Switzerland.

a) The principle of the use of different languages. Through the action of the Holy Spirit, the disciples "began to speak in other tongues," and the multitude that gathered on that occasion was bewildered, "because each one heard them speaking in his own language" (Acts 2:1-9). On that day it was revealed that the gospel, so as to be understood by those who are the hearers, must be proclaimed in their "own language."

We know that the church has not always and in every place been obedient to this revelation. Even today language is often a significant obstacle to the hearing and understanding of the gospel. At times the institutional church *insists* on the proclamation of the good news in a language that is foreign and unknown to the hearers. This is a direct and deliberate contradiction of the spirit of pentecost.

b) The second principle deals with race. When some questions arose among the first disciples about preaching to and baptizing gentiles, a vision revealed to Peter by our Lord forced him to affirm: "Truly I perceive that God shows no particularity, but in every nation anyone who fears him and does what is right is acceptable to him" (Acts 10:34–35).

Again we must admit our failure through the ages to be obedient to this affirmation of the apostle Peter. Racism is rampant in the world today and often finds Christians among its strongest advocates. The church must continually reaffirm its opposition to racism and proclaim more forcefully and convincingly the gospel of love and justice for all.

c) The third principle deals with culture and was best expressed by St Paul: "To the Jews I became like a Jew, to win the Jews. To those under the law I became like one under the law, though I myself am not under the law, so as to win those under the law . . . To the weak I became weak to win the weak. I have become all things to all men so that by all possible means I might save some. I do all this for the sake of the gospel, that I may share in its blessings" (I Cor. 9:20-23).

Too often those bringing the gospel to a new context made no attempt to understand and immerse themselves in the culture. They rather sought to uproot and radically change that culture without any regard for its positive values. We must repeatedly reassert that this is in contradiction to the apostolic tradition.

16

3. LITURGY AND MISSION

Throughout history, the worship of the church has been the expression and guardian of divine revelation. Not only does it express and represent the saving events of Christ's life, death, resurrection and ascension to heaven, but it is also, for the members of the church, the living anticipation of the kingdom to come. In worship, the church, being the body of Christ enlivened by the Holy Spirit, unites the faithful as the adopted sons and daughters of God, the Father.

Liturgical worship is an action of the church and is centred around the eucharist. Although the sacrament of the eucharist, since the very origin of the church, was a celebration closed to outsiders, and full participation in the eucharist remains reserved for the members of the church, liturgical worship as a whole is an obvious form of witness and mission.

The Eucharistic Liturgy as a Missionary Event

The eucharistic liturgy is the full participation of the faithful in the salvation brought about by the incarnation of the divine Logos and through them into the whole cosmos. By the mutual self-giving of Christ and of his people, by sanctification of the bread and wine and the "christification" of the communicants, it is the place where we experience the fullness of salvation, the communion of the Holy Spirit, heaven on earth. Through the humble and "kenotic" hiding of the divine word in the mystery of the bread, offered, broken, and given, "we proclaim his death and confess his resurrection until he comes again."

It is the role of the eucharistic liturgy to initiate us into the kingdom, to enable us to "taste . . . and see that the Lord is good" (Ps. 34:8, quoted by I Pet. 2:3). It is the function of the liturgy to transform us as individuals into "living stones" of the church and as a community into an authentic image of the kingdom.

The liturgy is our thanksgiving for – and on behalf of – the created world, and the restoration in Christ of the fallen world. It is the image of the kingdom; it is the *cosmos* becoming *ecclesia*.

Liturgy as Preparation for Witness

The divine liturgy – divine because, though celebrated by human beings, it is essentially the work of God – begins with a cry of joy and gratitude: "Blessed is the kingdom of the Father, Son and Holy Spirit." The entire eucharistic liturgy unfolds within the horizon of the kingdom, which is its *raison d'être* and its goal.

This kingdom is a dynamic reality: it has come and it is coming, because Christ has come and Christ is coming. The mission of the church will therefore be to summon people of all nations and of all ages to become a pilgrim people. The liturgy is an invitation to join with the Lord and to travel with him. This appears at the beginning of the Orthodox liturgies in the Little Entrance with the gospel and in the Great Entrance with the offering of bread and wine: "In thy kingdom. Remember us, O Lord, when thou comest in thy kingdom . . . May the Lord God remember us all in his kingdom . . ." This movement of the liturgy carries us along with Christ towards the promised land.

The kingdom, prepared for us before the creation of the world (Matt. 25:34) and proclaimed in the whole of Christ's preaching, was given to the world by the Lamb of God offering himself on the cross and by his rising again from the dead. In its liturgy, the church gives thanks ("makes eucharist,") for this gift, in the words: "Thou . . . hast left nought undone till thou hadst brought us into heaven and bestowed upon us thy kingdom for to come." By its thanksgiving, by its eucharist, the church receives the gift of the kingdom.

In the liturgy, we all "by participating in the one bread and one chalice" ask "to be united in the communion of the one Holy Spirit" (Lit. St. Basil) standing before the one holy table led by one bishop, we pray together as brothers and sisters of Christ to our common Father. Our distinct persons, united by love, confess with one mind the unity of the three divine persons, Father, Son and Holy Spirit, consubstantial and indivisible trinity.

The gift given by the Son in his self-offering on the cross is communicated to people of all times by the Holy Spirit who receives what belongs to the Son and communicates it to us (cf. John 16:14). When the Holy Spirit is invoked in the prayer of epiclesis, the celebrant prays: "that thy Holy Spirit may come upon us and upon these gifts . . . that they may be to them that partake thereof unto sobriety of soul, the remission of sins, the participation of thy Holy Spirit, the fulfillment of the kingdom of heaven . . ." In the course of the liturgy, the radiance of the Holy Spirit projects the full image of the kingdom onto the church gathered together by him. The liturgy is the continuation of pentecost. When all the faithful come to communicate, they enter into the splendour of the kingdom.

Immediately after we have in this way met with him who has come but whom we also expect to come again, we cry out: "Grant that we may partake of thee more truly, in that day of thy kingdom which shall have no night." Everything is given to us in this communion yet everything is not yet accomplished. The efficacy of the church's missionary witness depends on the authenticity of our communion. Our ability to present the light of the kingdom to the world is proportionate to the degree in which we receive it in the eucharistic mystery.

Although the eucharist is the most perfect access to the economy of salvation, it is the goal – and also the springboard – of mission, rather than the means of mission. The eucharist reveals the iconic function of the church. The church as institution points to the eucharistic assembly as its sole genuine image, as the transparent icon of Christ.

Worship as the Motivating Factor of Life

Worship is the centre of the life of the church, but it should also determine the whole life of every Christian. "Every tree that does not bear good fruit is cut down and thrown into the fire. Thus you will know them by their fruits. Not every one who says to me 'Lord, Lord' shall enter the kingdom of heaven, but he who does the will of my Father who is in heaven" (Matt. 7:20-23). The realization of these words of Christ has a great significance for the success of Christian mission.

The human person, through membership in the worshipping community, in spiritual poetry, in church music, in iconography, with body and soul (I Cor. 6:20), actively participates in the gifts of grace. This involvement of human nature in its fullness – and not only of reason – in glorifying God, is an essential factor of Orthodox worship. It must be

19

preserved and developed, as a powerful means of Christian witness.

The Priest and the Liturgy
In order to become a really powerful expression of the church's mission in the world, worship must be meaningfully understood by its participants (I Cor. 14:6-15). It is through a full participation in the liturgy that the people realize both the teaching and then the life, death and resurrection of Jesus Christ, which is the very reality of what we are attempting to proclaim. In other words, the liturgy itself is the proclamation of the gospel in an existential and experiential manner. This has certain implications for the Orthodox priest.
– The liturgy is not for the priest alone, i.e. it is not he alone who celebrates, but rather the entire people of God (clergy and laity) who celebrate. It is in his *function* only, given in ordination, that he is to lead the people in the liturgy.
– The priest must never separate the *kerygma* of Christ, i.e. the teaching, proclamation, and exhortation of the scripture, from the liturgy; this kerygma is part of the very fabric of the liturgy. There is an analogy of this link between the teaching and the sacrifice (*anaphora*) and the eating (*koinonia*), to be seen in the life of our Lord when he *first* taught the people and then offered himself in his body and blood on behalf of all.
– Thus, preaching, being an essential part of worship, should never be omitted, whatever the number of those present at every occasion.
– Through sermons and homilies, the priest must adapt the words of the Scripture to the reality of the circumstances. Noting the difference between relativity and relevance, it is important that this adaptation be made without changing the essential, life-giving, and salvatory message. For this, there is thus a constant need for proper training and preparation vis-à-vis the sermon.

The Participation of the Faithful
Because the liturgy is proclamation, it is imperative that the people of God participate in this reality.
– The parish members must be educated to understand what it is that is happening in the divine liturgy, and in this way to comprehend the proclamation in the liturgy.

– Among the means of achieving the participation of a greater number of faithful in the liturgical life of the church, there should be, wherever possible, a greater involvement of the laity, including women, in those forms of worship that are allowed to them by the church, especially in congregational singing. All people, children and adults, men and women, should learn the hymns of the liturgy. In order to facilitate this, the liturgy should be in the language of the land (which is comprehensive and contemporary) and thus encourage the active and conscientious participation of the people.

– There are aspects of the liturgy that may make it appear frozen and irrelevant. It is thus necessary to make the liturgical language more accessible to the average faithful, and it might be desirable to take initiatives (with the blessing of ecclesiastical authorities) that would make our forms of worship more comprehensible to young people (for example, catechetical explanations could precede the services).

– The important educative role of the icon and of liturgical art in general, in an initiation into an understanding of the mysteries of the church and of faith, cannot be overstressed.

– The church seeks to order our whole life by the sanctification of time, by the liturgical cycles, the celebration of the year's festivals, the observance of fasts, the practice of ascesis, and regular visitation. An effort must be made to bring into everyday life the liturgical rhythm of the consecration of time (matins, hours, vespers, saints' days, feast days).

– New forms of worship patterned on the old ones should be developed, having in mind the special needs of contemporary society (i.e. of travellers, youth, children, people in industry). Also, wherever that is possible, the establishment of new worshipping communities, outside the existing parishes and temples, could be considered.

– The church should seriously study the renewal of the ancient tradition of the Order of Deaconess, as this is mentioned in early ecumenical councils.

As in the days following pentecost, a sharing "community" must be created to make the whole church a practising "community of the saints and a holy nation," for it is in the ever-living communion of the saints that the church's faith is experienced and passed on in its most intense and purest form.

Liturgical Spirituality and Witness

It belongs to the very nature of the church to bear witness to the gospel in the world. This witness is rooted in the coming of the Spirit at pentecost. From pentecost until the parousia, the risen Christ is made manifest and present by the Holy Spirit in liturgical life, through word and sacraments. The whole life and prayer of the church's members, whether meeting together for common worship or celebrating each one "in the temple of the heart," centres on the eucharist. Here all the prayers and liturgical acts of the people of God converge; here the church discovers its true identity. In all of Christian spirituality, eucharistic spirituality creates a dynamic piety, mystical bonds with Christ that overcome evil by realizing fully the mystery of incarnation and divinization in all its dimensions. The eucharistic human being is in fact a human being who overcomes the conditioning of our fallen nature.

In the liturgical celebration, which extends into the daily life of the church's members, the church announces and achieves the advent of the kingdom of the holy trinity. In all things, it commemorates the glorified Christ and gives thanks to God in Jesus Christ. The entire tradition of the church, its worship, its theology, and its preaching, is a doxology, a continual thanksgiving, a confession of faith in Christ's Easter triumph and our liberation from all the forces that oppress and degrade us.

– Prayer and the eucharist, whereby Christians overcome their selfish ways, impel them also to become involved in the social and political life of their respective countries.

– The faithful should, as well, establish personal contact with non-believers, in order to transmit the spiritual experiences gained by a meaningful participation in the liturgy.

– Orthodox spirituality is a spirituality that embraces the great variety of ways whereby human life is sanctified and which, through fasting and ascesis, makes it possible for us to participate in the divine life both physically and with the whole range of our faculties. This sanctification also includes the human mind, in which its arrogant self-sufficiency is conquered and illumination granted to it in the confession of faith and in the act of praise. Orthodox spirituality is thus a tried and tested school in which human beings are initiated into the mystery of God, the mystery of God's love and of God's salvation accomplished and communicated. This understanding is given and received by various forms of spiritual and pastoral guidance, by confession, and it culminates in the authentic creation of a new life by the Holy Spirit, a life in which "it is no longer I that live but Christ lives in me."

– The common spirituality of the people of God and monastic spirituality must not be treated as if these were mutually opposed. Nor must we restrict to just a few people the continual invocation of the blessed name of Jesus. In Orthodoxy great value is attached to the plurality of forms and expressions of Christian devotion. At every stage in their spiritual journey, Christians receive the gifts of the Holy Spirit in rich measure and can achieve the perfection to which they are called.

4. HOLY SCRIPTURE, PROCLAMATION AND LITURGY

The Bible and the liturgy must not be isolated as self-contained, autonomous entities. They were established to remain together, united forever.

The Interaction of the Bible and Liturgical Life

The liturgical life of the church is one of the most fundamental ways in which it proclaims the word of God to the world. It is especially in and through the liturgy and divine services that people come to know God as manifested and still being manifest to the world in Jesus Christ. Our Lord Jesus Christ, crucified, risen and ascended, is the unchanging content and message of the gospel and of the liturgy (I Cor. 1:23; I Cor. 15:20; Mark 16:19).

Holy scripture is the source and basis of the whole liturgical and spiritual life of the church. The Bible contains the revealed message of the old and new covenants. This message finds its liturgical actualization in the worship of the church, especially in the eucharist, the sacrament of the new covenant. In the course of the liturgical year, through feasts, readings, sermons, biblical instruction, hymnography, symbols and iconography, the church actualizes the mystery of the history of salvation and renews the covenant between God and God's people.

– The biblical content and understanding of the liturgy must constantly be reaffirmed, so that they are not distorted by merely folkloristic, ritualistic or cultural attitudes. Within the liturgy, the proclamation of the good news is not just an evangelistic event. It also becomes an ecclesial reality through the eucharistic communion. The church is the eucharistic manifestation of the history of salvation, which is witnessed to and made evident in the New Testament. It is therefore crucial for Christians to understand their life and history in the perspective of the holy scriptures. This points to the ecclesial reality itself and to the eucharistic status of the church. Orthodoxy cannot dissociate the biblical vision of the church from its liturgical manifestation.

– The proclamation of the word receives its full theological significance and power within the assembly, the visible manifestation of the eucharistic community. The incarnate word of God nourishes the church in the liturgy, as good news and as spiritual bread. Indeed, one cannot share in the eucharistic part of the liturgy without fully sharing in its kerygmatic part (biblical readings, sermons, etc.). In the liturgy the participant is guided by the book of life on the way to a full knowledge of divine revelation.

– Both in the gospel and in the liturgy, Jesus Christ is continually offering himself as "the way, the truth, and the life" (John 14:6). Because the liturgy is founded on the word of God and is permeated by it, it is of particular importance for evangelistic witness.

– The Bible occupies a unique place in the liturgy, filling it with deep meaning. The liturgy becomes a living word of God addressed to people; it creates an atmosphere of dialogue between a person and God and between persons. In the liturgy we talk with God and God talks with us; we pray to God, we thank and glorify God. Through our prayer, thanksgiving and praise we proclaim God. Therefore the liturgy is indeed a proclamation.

Biblical and Liturgical Language

Because of the special place of the Bible in the liturgical life of the church, it should become more understandable and accessible to the people: ". . . the sheep hear his voice, and he calls his own sheep by name and leads them out . . . and the sheep follow him, for they know his voice. A stranger they will not follow, but they will flee from him, for they do not know the voice of strangers" (John 10:3-5).

Attention must be given to both biblical and liturgical language, for this is a crucial challenge for the Orthodox witness of today. This problem has two aspects: on the one hand, in many Orthodox churches, through the old biblical and liturgical texts, a national language and culture was shaped and is still protected. On the other, the old liturgical language limits the very possibilities of the contemporary faithful to identify themselves with the liturgy, which is their prayer, and handicaps the church in communicating with the younger generation.

Thus, in preaching and in the liturgy, it is of utmost importance that the Bible be communicated to people in their mother tongue and in a language that they can understand: ". . . But if I do not know the meaning of the language, I shall be a foreigner to the speaker and the speaker a foreigner to me" (I Cor. 14:11). "I could wish to be present with you now and to change my tone . . ." (Gal. 4:20). Every Christian should have direct access to the text of the holy scriptures both through private and liturgical readings.

Finally, in renewing the question of language, each Orthodox Church should take into account its local, cultural, historical and psychological setting as well as pastoral needs.

A Greater Access to the Word of God

– It is important that the faithful have a better knowledge of, and a more direct access to, the biblical texts printed wholly or in part in the language they speak. The translation and distribution of the Bible remains an important task and responsibility of the church.

– It would be worthwhile to have the entire text of the Bible (Old and New Testaments) read during the liturgical Sunday synaxes and to improve the pericopes of evangelical and apostolic readings prescribed for the Sundays and feasts of the year. For in these days multitudes of God's people assemble who, because of the incompleteness and monotony of the pericope, are deprived of the possibility to listen to the word of God and its interpretation in its fullness. This will not only result in a better common knowledge of the Bible but in the enrichment and renewal of the topics treated in the homilies.

– So that we might participate more fully in the all-sanctifying and illuminating power of divine grace which is communicated in the liturgy and through the word of God, a more extensive reading of the Bible in liturgies not combined directly with the eucharist should be promoted. In this respect, the church should consider reinstituting the old practice of using a variety of liturgies, whose styles reflect the missionary milieux and the culture of the participants.

– All possible assistance should be provided to those who stimulate interest for Bible studies among people, under the guidance of the church.

– Another way of bringing the good news closer to people is to illustrate the various important Bible stories by using icons that are venerated by the people: ". . . every scribe who has been trained for the kingdom of heaven is like a householder who brings out of his treasure what is new and what is old" (Matt. 13:52).

– In order to communicate with a society where contacts with the church's liturgical life are becoming increasingly rare, churches can use the methods and means offered by modern technology. Their use should be carefully studied as well as the message that is communicated through them.

Proclamation and Interpretation

Throughout its history, the church has continued the ministry of the apostles by following the command of Jesus Christ (Matt. 28:19-20). It has been called to celebrate the holy mysteries and to proclaim the gospel to all nations. Thus, the duty to preach is part of the Christian priesthood just as are both sacramental actions and pastoral ministry.

The Bible is alive in the liturgy. It is opened to the people through the lips of the praying church. The word of God becomes alive and effective through proclamation and interpretation in the sermon, which is an integral part of the liturgy, and it transforms the inner life of the listener.

– One of the principal aims of preaching the word of God is to give an interpretation, under the guidance of the Holy Spirit, of biblical events in ways which meet the spiritual needs of people today and which speak to problems confronting them.

– In his preaching, the priest should respond not only to the personal and religious questions of the faithful, but also to their present social concerns.

– There is a need for the renewal of the preaching and teaching ministry, especially in view of the concerns and problems of the new audience of the worship services. Because the celebrant is both priest and preacher, the church should give the utmost importance, in the education of the clergy, to the teaching of the Bible, homiletics, catechetics and liturgics in view of the ministry of the word (Acts 6:4). The priest must learn to adapt his proclamation and teaching to his listeners, avoiding ecclesiastical verbiage, and taking into account the language used in his missionary environment.

– As an example of this, the patristic homilies are an excellent model for preaching today. This type of sermon actualizes the message of the biblical text in a pastoral and communal perspective and puts the emphasis on God's action in the history and life of men and women. Such homilies should be simple, short, authentic, and reflect the inner dialogue between the preacher and the faithful. They should enable the truth of God to manifest itself in and through the weakness of human language.

– Any other creative ways of preaching the Bible already existing within local Orthodox churches should be regarded as valuable and as deserving further dissemination.

Proclamation to the World

We must remain conscious of our responsibility before God, the church and all humanity to fulfil the commandment of our Lord Jesus Christ: ". . . Go, therefore, and make disciples of all peoples . . ." (Matt. 28:19). It also follows from the way the great apostle to the Gentiles felt about it in saying ". . . Woe to me if I do not preach the gospel!" (I Cor. 9:16). ". . . He who speaks in a tongue, should pray for the power to interpret. For if I pray in a tongue, my spirit prays but my mind is unfruitful" (I Cor. 14:13-14).

Today, however, our witness is handicapped by the erosion of the sense of the sacred in the contemporary world. The proclamation and the teaching of holy scripture must take into account the social and cultural realities of society in order to become accessible and understandable. The hearers of this proclamation and teaching will then be able to discover, through the liturgy, the true spiritual and sacred dimension of this world, which is often hidden by difficult terminology.

Liturgy and Proclamation

Proclamation should not be taken only in the narrow sense of an informative preaching of the truth, but rather of incorporating humanity into the mystical union with God. At every step of the liturgy we encounter the word of God. Although they belong chronologically to the past, the saving events of divine economy, through the Holy Spirit's action, transcend time's limitation, become really present, and the faithful in the here and now live that which historically belongs to the past, as well as to the eschaton. In the liturgy we do not have simply a memorial, but a living reality. It is an epicletic contemporization and consecration. A continuous parousia, a real presence of Christ emerges through the liturgy.

To Whom is the Gospel Proclaimed?

The incarnation was for the whole people of all ages and for the redemption of the whole cosmos. The holy eucharist was instituted, among other things, to proclaim the death and the resurrection of our Lord "until he comes again." Thus, the following categories of people should directly or indirectly hear the message of the holy eucharist.

– The members of the church who try sincerely to practise the faith should be made true evangelists by the gospel proclaimed to them. St. John Chrysostom said: "I do not believe in the salvation of anyone who does not try to save others."

– The nominal Christians who attend the church just as a routine.

– The mobile population, migrant workers, refugees, etc., some of whom have no permanent roots under the sun.

– People of the diaspora of our modern age.

– The non-Christians in the vicinity of our congregations and churches who are still to a large extent strangers to the healing and radiating power of the gospel.

– The fields where no one has ever preached the gospel.

How do we Proclaim the Gospel?

During the liturgy the readings from the Bible are done not as self-centred service and action, but in the service of the liturgical life of the church. To accomplish the mission of the church in proclaiming the gospel, a variety of methods and approaches must be used, according to the possibilities and the needs of the local church.

– The faithful should have continual education in understanding the meaning of the liturgy and the message of the gospel.

– Meaningful literature should be published, such as: informative pamphlets; pictorial and illustrated publications; volumes of new homilies and sermons, etc.

– The mass media of television, radio, and newspapers should be employed.

– Theological training of priests must emphasize the importance of an awareness of the needs for pastoral care, missionary zeal, and the proclamation of the word.

5. THE GOOD NEWS
AND EVANGELISTIC WITNESS

What is Evangelistic Witness?

Evangelistic witness is not the whole mission of the church, which has many other dimensions. Evangelistic witness is here understood to be the communication of Christ to those who do not consider themselves Christian, wherever these people may be found. This includes the need of the church to witness to some of its own nominal members.

By its nature, however, evangelistic witness is first of all and primarily a confrontation of humankind by the message, judgement, love, presence, redemption, command and transfiguring power of the energies of the one, holy and undivided trinity.

Evangelistic witness is a call to salvation, which means the restoration of the relationship of God and humanity, as understood in the Orthodox teaching of *theosis*. This message has its source in the scriptures, which witness to the redemption of humankind in Christ Jesus, yet it also includes a worldview which locates each of us *vis-à-vis* God, our fellows as individuals and in society, as well as our own personhood and destiny. It includes both the relationship of God and each person, and the relationship of human being to fellow human being (vertical and horizontal).

Evangelistic witness brings to each the true response to the essential need *qua* human being. It is the bringing of the divine response to the real need of persons as individuals and of persons in community. It is the message of human restoration and the divinization of the human. As such it speaks to the most profound human need, yet it also meets and overcomes the felt needs of human beings in more specific and concrete dimensions.

Because human beings are fallen, evangelistic witness will also appear to have an element of foolishness (*moria*), and will always contain within it an element of *skandalon* simply because human wisdom cannot fully comprehend the transcendent wisdom of God. Yet, evangelistic witness does more than provide a message of divine dimensions; it also conveys a way of living applicable in full within the community of the body of believers, the church, and in part in the world at large.

Why are we Required to Make Evangelistic Witness?

We do not have the option of keeping the good news to ourselves. Sharing the word and communicating the word and confessing the faith once given to the saints is an integral part of fulfilling the image and likeness of God and the achievement of *theosis*. Like St. Paul, the believer must be able to say about all who do not know the life in Christ what he said about his fellow countrymen: ". . . my heart's desire and prayer to God for them is that they may be saved" (Rom. 10:1). The uncommunicated gospel (good news) is a patent contradiction.

The goal of evangelistic witness – though it may pass through many stages and pause at many intermediate places – is finally one: conversion from a life characterized by sin, separation from God, submission to evil and the unfulfilled potential of God's image, to a new life characterized by the forgiveness of sins, obedience to the commands of God, renewed fellowship with God in the trinity, growth in the restoration of the divine image, and the realization among us of the prototype of the love of Christ. More briefly and succinctly put, the final goal of evangelistic witness is conversion and baptism. Conversion is a wilful turning from sin, death and evil to true life in God. Baptism is the reception of a new member into the new life of the community of God's people, the church.

Though the conversion and baptism of all is the final goal of evangelistic witness, there is a need to identify many intermediate goals also, such as:

– the increase of love and dialogue among Christians and non-Christians;
– the formation of the gospel message into the language and thought-forms of the non-Christian neighbour;
– the interpenetration of the structures of society;
– the promulgation of the will of God in reference to the injustice among us; and
– the prophetic challenge to the world's values.

All these share in the task of evangelistic witness and in part serve as a motive to speak the word of Christ to all.

Who Performs the Task of Evangelistic Witness?

The most true and profound response to this question would be that it is God, through the power of the Holy Spirit, who does the work of evangelistic witness. We are made *diakonoi* of the gospel, "according to the gift of God's grace which was given [us] by the working of his power" (Eph. 3:7). In a further sense, it is the whole community of God which does this work.

The clergy

More particularly, four groups or classes of Christians are charged, each in their own way, with the task of evangelistic witness. First are those ordained in the Lord's service. The chief evangelist of the church is the bishop with his presbyterion and diaconate as well as the monastic establishment. In the history of the church, these "professionals" of evangelistic witness have carried on this work for the church with great success. And inasmuch as they still lead the worship, preach the word of God, visit the oppressed and suffering, speak the word of truth in the tribunals of power, proclaim the gospel before vast audiences electronically present, communicate the Orthodox truth through the printed word, or walk the foreign mission trails, they continue to do so. Yet, we are all too conscious of our lethargy and deafness to the divine commission. Theological schools of all levels are challenged to heal that deafness through proper and full education for evangelical witness of the candidates for Holy Orders. There is a need to restore the claim of evangelical witness upon the priestly conscience of these servants of God.

The priest as evangelist

"Evangelist," which differs from catechist, here means one who must "go forth and proclaim the gospel," i.e. to both nominal Christians, the "potential parish," and to non-believers. This, however, presents various problems with which the Orthodox must deal.

It is within the very nature of the faith that the *Evangelion* as a "witness" to Jesus Christ must be emphasized. In various cultures, this must be done with whatever means are available to the priest.

Here the personality of the priest is crucial in the sense that he must have proper respect for others, possess an

ment have provided humankind with an enviable control over the conditions of life. Yet that control has had many undesirable consequences, also. It has taught people to think of themselves primarily as consumers; they are *homo economicus*. Their circumscribed goals of life require no transcendent referent, no forgiveness, no restoration of relationship, no sacramental life, no *theosis*, no God. Yet, exactly because they sit in that darkness, they are the object of the church's evangelistic witness.

Institutions of modern society
Evangelistic witness will also speak to the structures of this world, its economic, political and societal institutions. Especially necessary is the witness of social justice in the name of the poor and the oppressed. We must re-learn the patristic lesson that the church is the mouth and voice of the poor and the oppressed in the presence of the powers that be.

In our own way we must learn once again "how to speak to the ear of the King," on the people's behalf.

How do we Make our Evangelistic Witness?
It is the task of evangelistic witness to lead persons to the acknowledgement of God's saving power in their lives. "[He] is the Lord of all and bestows his riches upon all who call upon him." Yet, "how are men to call upon him in whom they have not believed? And how are they to believe in him of whom they have never heard? And how are they to hear without a preacher? And how can men preach unless they are sent?" (Rom. 10:12, 14-15). After two thousand years this Pauline injunction retains its urgency and timeliness.

Yet those same intervening years require us to review our conceptions of the methods of evangelistic witness. On the one hand it is clear that proclamation alone is not the only way in which evangelistic witness is made. Further, in this day and age mere preaching may no longer be the most effective way of evangelistic witness. Paul does not tell us what we are to do when the gospel has been proclaimed and rejected, or even worse, simply ignored! Yet, of one thing we are sure. We are sent by Christ to bear witness to him and his saving truth for all of humankind.

Prerequisites for Witness

Faith and humility

How is it to be done today? In the first instance this question must be directed to the attitudes and motives of "those who are sent." Those who are sent must first be conscious of their own repentance, conversion and salvation. Those who are fully aware of the new life of grace in the community of the holy trinity and in the reality of the community of the church alone are able to communicate the saving witness. This comes about above all with the knowledge that nothing we do is of effect without the energizing power of the trinity. No matter what it is that we do in evangelistic witness we know that it is "God making his appeal through us" (II Cor. 5:20).

As difficult and beyond our capabilities as the work of evangelistic witness may seem, then, we undertake the task with a spirit not of fear or of inadequacy or of insufficiency – though all these in truth exist in us – but with hope that through our meagre efforts this witness may be empowered by the gracious energies of the triune God, in whose name we undertake the task.

And so it is that "those who are sent" to be evangelistic witnesses do so as ones having experienced the redemption of God and who then work with the full understanding of their own insufficiency, fully expecting the grace of God to "provide the growth." Thus it is in a constant spirit of *metanoia* (repentance), with a full sense of our own limitations that we make our evangelistic witness.

Koinonia and love

How is evangelistic witness to be made today objectively? The chief means of witness for the church today is not the bold announcement of Christ as saviour to a world which has already heard the words and still remains unresponsive. The first and chief method of evangelistic witness is the same as that of the early church. Those who saw the quality of life of those early believers were so attracted by its power and beauty that they sought to find its power and its source (e.g. Epistle of Diognetus; Libanus' praise of Chrysostom's mother).

Thus, the first method of evangelistic witness is the sharing of love by those who have acknowledged the love of God for them. "We love because he first loved us" (I John 4:19).

It was an injunction to evangelistic witness when the apostle of love instructed: "Beloved, let us love one another; for love is of God, and he who loves is born of God and knows God" (I John 4:7).

More specifically, the same apostle says, ". . . this is the love of God, that we keep his commandments . . . this is the victory that overcomes the world, our faith" (I John 5:3-4). Our obedience to God's will is a powerful form of evangelistic witness as well. We have cheapened the gospel in the past by much talking and little practice. Our obedience to God's will must now be the vehicle for our message.

The call to justice and truth
But the word of God cannot be contained only in the personal sphere. Evangelistic witness must also be made before the social and political tribunal. Christians must address the word of God to contemporary issues of justice with all available means. Evangelistic witness must keep a vigilant eye upon all emergent social movements and concerns (women's liberation, racial consciousness, sexual freedom, etc.) in order to speak the word of truth. But it should seek to do its task toward and in these situations not by parroting words of another age, but by reformulating the unchanging truth with an eye to its contemporization. Certainly, in doing this it will also respond creatively in the patristic spirit to the ever-new and ever-changing phenomena of our times.

6. MISSION AS
"LITURGY AFTER THE LITURGY"

The Liturgy As a Means of Personal Growth

The liturgy is not an escape from life, but a continuous transformation of life according to the prototype of Jesus Christ, through the power of the Spirit.

If it is true that in the liturgy we do not only hear a message but we also anticipate in the great event of liberation from sin our communion with the person of Christ through the real presence of the Holy Spirit, then this event of our personal incorporation into the body of Christ, this transfiguration of our little being into a member of Christ, must be evident and be proclaimed in all our life. The liturgy has to be continued in personal everyday situations. Every one of the faithful is called upon to continue a secret devotion, on the secret altar of the heart, to realize a living proclamation of the good news "for the sake of the whole world." Without this continuation the liturgy remains half finished. Since by the eucharistic event we are incorporated in Christ to serve the world and be sacrificed for it, we have to express in concrete *diakonia*, in community life, our new being in Christ, who is the servant of all. The sacrifice of the eucharist must be extended in personal sacrifices for people in need, the brothers and sisters for whom Christ died. Since the liturgy is the participation in the great event of liberation from the demonic powers, then the continuation of liturgy in life means a continuous liberation from the powers of evil that are working inside us (e.g. the terrible complex of egoism), a continual re-orientation and openness to insights and efforts aiming at liberating human persons from all demonic structures of injustice, exploitation, agony and loneliness, and aiming at creating real communion of persons in love.

The Witness of the Community In the World

The liturgy does not end when the eucharistic assembly disperses. "Let us go forth in peace"; the dismissal is a sending off of every believer to mission in the world where he or she lives and works, and of the whole community into the world, to witness by what they are that the kingdom is coming. Christians who have heard the word and received the bread of life should henceforth be living prophetic signs of the coming kingdom. Having been sanctified, for they have become temples of the Holy Spirit, and deified, because they have been kindled by the fire descended from heaven, they hear the exhortation: "Heal the sick . . . and say to them, 'the kingdom of God has come near to you . . . behold, I have given you authority to tread upon . . . all the power of the enemy' " (Luke 10:9-19). Every Christian is called to proclaim the kingdom and to demonstrate its power. Hence a manifold function:

– The exorcism of demons: the struggle against the idols of racism, money, nationalism, ideologies, and the robotization and exploitation of human beings.

– The healing of the sick: the church exercises this function not only in the sacraments of penance and the anointing of the sick but also by tackling all the ills and disorders of the human being and society. It does this in the power of the cross: self-effacing service of the sick and prisoners; solidarity with the tortured and the oppressed, especially with those who suffer for their opinions. As the voice of the voiceless, the church must, in the discharge of its calling, teach and practice respect for every human being, with the aim of restoring the divine image in each individual and communion among all. It should encourage respect for the whole of creation and everything in nature. A kingdom of priests, it offers up the whole of creation – obedient to Christ and renewed by the Spirit – to God the Father.

– Voluntarily accepted poverty in demonstration of solidarity with the poor king (cf. Zech. 9:9).

– Fasting with him who said that "man does not live by bread alone," "for the kingdom of God does not mean food and drink but righteousness and peace and joy, in the Holy Spirit" (Rom. 14:17).

– Identification with all those who go hungry.

– Chastity not only in monastic life but also in conjugal love and procreation.

– Revaluation of the humility which makes it possible for the other person to be renewed.

– Mutual submission (cf. Eph. 5:21) in listening to the Spirit who speaks through the church.

– A liberty which refuses to let itself be intimidated by threats or taken in by false promises.
– Constant interior prayer throughout all the vicissitudes of daily life.
All these are aspects of a life based on an eschatological vision of existence, on an evangelical life worthy of the children of the kingdom.

The Parish and Mission
Although the essence of Christian mission is the proclamation to each human being of the gospel of forgiveness, resurrection and life eternal, such proclamation is valid, credible and effective only if it is not isolated from the gospel of love, by which Christians are recognized as Christ's disciples, from involvement and sharing in suffering wherever it may appear. For mission is the work of the same Holy Spirit that anointed Christ "to preach good news to the poor, to proclaim release to the captives and recovering of sight to the blind, to set at liberty those who are oppressed, to proclaim the acceptable year of the Lord" (Luke 4:18-19).

While preaching the gospel of the eternal kingdom that is yet to come, we know that this kingdom is already present in our midst and is realized every time we sacrifice ourselves for the will of God to be done on earth as it is in heaven.

The missionary character of the parish is rooted in its very nature. Although administratively and institutionally it is a part of the church, sacramentally and spiritually it possesses the fulness of the gifts of the Holy Spirit; it is indeed the presence and epiphany of the whole church, of the whole faith, and of the whole grace. As the whole church, the parish is called to preach and to teach the saving gospel of Christ in the world and to be the witness of Christ in the particular conditions set for it by God. In this sense the entire life of the parish is a mission, for it exists not merely for the religious edification of its members, but above all for the salvation of the whole world from the power of the "prince of this world."

The living source of the fulfillment by the parish of this mission is the liturgy whose very essence is the epiphany and the communication of the kingdom of God revealed in the life, the teaching, the death, the resurrection, and the glorification of Jesus Christ. The meaning of the liturgy has often been obscured by one-sided interpretations, in which it was presented almost exclusively as a means of individual sanctification. It is urgent, therefore, that we rediscover the initial *lex orandi* of the church in its cosmic, redemptive and eschatological dimensions. Behind this static and individualistic understanding of the liturgy we must recover its dynamic nature and power. It edifies and fulfils the church as the sacrament of the kingdom; it transforms us, the members of the church, into the witnesses of Christ, and his co-workers.

The Role of the Laity
Together with the rediscovery of the essential meaning of the liturgy, we must rediscover the true nature and vocation of the laity in the church. For too long the very term *laikos* carried with it connotations of passivity, of not belonging to the active, i.e. clerical, stratum in the church. But we know that initially the term meant the belonging to the laos, the people of God – to "a chosen race, a royal priesthood, a holy nation, God's own people," whom God "has called out of darkness into his marvelous light" (I Pet. 2:9). In the sacraments of baptism and holy chrismation, each member of the church was made into the temple of the Holy Spirit, dedicated, consecrated to God and called to serve him. In other terms, each laikos is, above all, called to be a witness, i.e. an active participant in the church's mission in the world.

Today, in several parts of the world, the task of bearing testimony to Christ, of bringing new people from darkness into the marvellous light of knowing Christ, is performed primarily by the laity. This alone should encourage us to rediscover the true nature and vocation of the laity, their unique place in the overall missionary ministry of the church. And again, there is no better way to that discovery than the study of the church's *leitourgia* as truly *concelebration*, a corporate act in which each member of the church finds his or her place in the edification of the body of Christ.

"We are fellow-workers for God," declares St. Paul (I Cor. 3:9). Through human voices and human lives, Christ's call to follow him reverberates throughout the centuries. For those who take it seriously, this "service" of the divine word and the divine love entails a deep and permanent surrender of their lives. Christians who obey the word of their Lord must resist the temptation to overrate their own importance and to come between God and God's children. The service of God and God's word demands a radical exercise in self-renunciation and spiritual povery, the better to be able to serve God and one's brothers and sisters. What St. John the Baptist said of himself in relation to Christ must also be true of us: "He must increase, but I must decrease" (John 3:30). This way of voluntary impoverishment following the pattern of the "Poor Man" thus helps to liberate the inner person and to make him or her capable of receiving the diverse charisms of the Holy Spirit so that through this sanctification, community and communion are strengthened and developed among human beings.

* * * * *

This is the basis of the Orthodox theology of mission, to acquire the dynamic, the power of the Spirit of Christ. It is the Spirit who creates the languages, forms and methods of mission. With this in mind, the whole people of God is summoned to be a true sign of the kingdom of God. It must confess courageously that the future of the church will come only as a gift of him who is the Lord of the future.

Internal Mission

The life of love

If the missionary proclamation of the gospel of the kingdom is to reach human hearts, there must be a palpable and real correspondence between the word preached in the power and joy of the Holy Spirit and the actual life of the Christian community. The gap between the message and the life of the historical church and its members constitutes the most massive obstacle to the credibility of the gospel for our contemporaries. "See how these Christians love one another," declared an ancient Christian apologist. The love of Christians is the very substance as well as the radiance of the gospel. In the apostolic community of Jerusalem as well as in the communities founded by St. Paul, the sharing of material things and concern for the poor became the spontaneous and necessary expression of their experience of the trinitarian love which is disclosed in the life of the church. The sharing of material things and of life itself thus flows from eucharistic communion and constitutes one of its radical requirements. When the church identifies itself with the prayer of its saviour, "Your kingdom come," it must above all ask itself in a spirit of penitence how much the unworthiness of Christians acts as a screen hindering the radiance of Christ himself from shining through.

The efficacy of missionary witness will be directly proportionate to the Christian experience of the love of Christ. This love, says St. Paul, "controls us" (II Cor. 5:14). Once this flame of love sets one's heart ablaze, it prevents one from isolating oneself comfortably in one's own personal existence or that of one's community. The dismissal of the faithful at the end of the liturgy with the words "Go forth in peace!" does not mean that the liturgy is over, but that it is transposed into another form in which it continues, in the inner worship of the heart, in a life immersed in the daily life of human society. It is high time we overcame the very real temptation to make an absolute distinction between a spiritual life and a secular life. All human existence is sacred and remains within God's sight. It is within that existence that Christ's sovereignty purposes to be installed, so that no realm or aspect of human life may be abandoned to the forces of evil.

Christians thus experience in their own flesh and blood the inevitable tension between existence in the world and not belonging to the world. It is precisely because of the Christian's heavenly citizenship (cf. Heb. 13:14) that he or she is able to enter fully into the whole life of human society and to bring the light of Christ to bear on that life.

Service

Christ said, "Go ye therefore and make disciples of all nations, baptizing them in the name of the Father, and of the Son, and of the Holy Spirit" (Matt. 28:19). This means that together with worship other forms of Christian activity have great importance for mission, such as:

- preaching;
- publications;
- personal contacts;
- welfare;
- religious education;
- youth movements, and
- renewal of monastic life.

Each church should take advantage of these forms of mission if they are available to it.

Asceticism

Those who practice a spirituality of "Christian maximalism," renewal groups, religious orders, set us an example of mission. A joyful asceticism, whereby the old self is crucified with Christ so that the new self may rise with him and live for God (Rom. 6:5-11) carries the cross and resurrection of Christ into daily life; it develops all the potentialities of baptism and constitutes an essential sign of the coming kingdom.

Theological education
There is a need for a deep change in the very understanding of the place of theology in our church. For centuries theology was thought of as an exclusively clerical task. But the time has come for a declericalization of theology. If theology is, above all, the study of the saving truth, it is needed by all members of the church; it is their essential spiritual food. To become this, however, it must revise its language, forms, and methods; it must be made into a common concern of the church. This change is needed by both clergy and laity, so that edification in the church – in a manner still to be defined – might become a continuous process of absorbing the saving truth and thereby entering it.

Spiritual life
The church ensures the continuity and authenticity of prayer by the variety and richness of its liturgical and sacramental life. The life of the Christian, renewed by the Holy Spirit, is founded on prayer. Through prayer, Christians rediscover their deepest roots, their bond with life. In the spiritual life that it nourishes and prepares, the liturgical celebration finds its indispensable continuation.

Participation in the Eucharist
Of particular importance is the lay participation in the eucharist, and, in general, the sacramental discipline of the church. There are divergences and discrepancies in the churches, however, which reflect different theological traditions and require for their elimination deep theological, pastoral and spiritual investigation and effort. No revival of the parish as a truly liturgical community fulfilling itself at Christ's table in his kingdom is possible without a eucharistic revival, which alone can give life and integrate with one another the gifts and charisms of all members of the body of Christ.

Development of individual gifts
The whole church bears witness to the good news of the renewal of divine life in our fallen world. When the church rediscovers its essence as a fellowship, we begin to live as

the church and not simply in the church. The church then ceases to be an oppressive structure and becomes again for its members the Father's house, providing them with shelter and with the heavenly bread. Here individual gifts are developed in all their rich diversity – prayer, love, wisdom, testimony – all contributing to the upbuilding of the one body of Christ.

Specific Areas of Internal Mission

The role of women

What is the proper place of women in this church of Christ that is essentially a fellowship? In a time when equal rights are being affirmed, do we not have to remember that it is in the body of Christ that woman finds both her true place and the forms of service that accord with her nature and her gifts?

The church today cannot ignore the question that presses on the universal human conscience concerning the place and role of woman in society in general, the special difficulties that she faces in an industrial society in which she participates as man's equal in the development of society, but in which, in virtue of her special charisms, she helps to uphold and carry the church and bears children both for life and for the Spirit. The church cannot be content to leave to others the burden of solving these questions about the distinctive dignity of woman in keeping with her nature, and about her liberation from all bondage by the Spirit of Christ.

Human relationships

The problems presented by marriage, by the growing incidence of divorce, by the difficulties of human love in a hedonistically oriented society, can only be solved in the spirituality of a transfiguration of human nature, by the path of asceticism and spiritual combat, for this is the only way in which the demons by which our society is possessed can be exorcized.

Family

It must be emphasized that it is in large measure within the family cell that Christian life becomes a reality and the health of all nations is thus renewed. In face of contemporary threats to the very existence of the family, it should be remembered that it is within its setting that the spiritual worship and the proclamation of the word of God takes place day by day, that the priesthood of the parents, who offer their children to the divine light and who are thus the provisional representatives and mirrors of the divine parenthood and compassion, is exercised.

Youth
The confusion and difficulties of young people cannot fail to concern the church at the deepest levels of its pastoral mission. Because of the vulnerability of the young but also because of the dynamism and vigour that is naturally theirs, special care needs to be given to the guidance of young people as they face up to the immense problems of life, love, suffering, and the struggle for existence. The Orthodox Church has a vision and a profound experience of the problems of childhood and youth that it should share with all people of good will.

7. WITNESS AND SERVICE

The Church and the World

Nowadays large sectors of society are living outside the church. These are not only the non-believers or the mass of half-hearted Christians in our parishes, but those who have never known, or have lost the "sense of God," or who have lost the understanding of human values.

The news of the mass media has taken the place of prayer and been substituted for the need to listen to the voice of God. It is easy to observe how men and women of the twentieth century seek to find a substitute for the absolute in the arts, eroticism, drugs, technology. For this category of men and women the notion of God has become meaningless, the only reality and value being the world and the search for material progress. In this situation our words have become empty.

Therefore, it must be asked how the notion of church and world can be better related so that our mission in the modern world is improved. The church is commissioned to change this worldly attitude to life, without forgetting that the human person and human dignity cannot be known fully without an authentic biblical revelation. It is the church's duty to affirm that the same world, where God is present and acting, does not lack the signs of the breath of the Holy Spirit. Sanctity and hope still sustain the health of this world and are still capable of liberating humanity, which has become unhinged because of its anguish, and of leading it back to God, the only source of joy and peace.

The church's mission aims at overcoming the divisions that prevail in the social and natural world by pointing to the event of communion that God offers to the world as the body of Christ, the church. The specificity, however, of the church's mission must never be lost sight of. It lies in the following main areas.

– Social transformation does justice to the church's mission provided that it fully respects each human being as a person, free and unique.

– Social transformation can make sense ultimately if the entire natural cosmos is transformed and death is abolished.
– Although the historical process cannot produce or bring about the kingdom of God, concern for the actual problems of human existence and the struggle for social justice constitute part of the "narrow gate" to that kingdom.

The Struggle against Poverty and Oppression

The dynamic of the church's mission springs from a deep awareness of the suffering of a human race steeped in ignorance of God, torn apart by hatred and conflict of every sort, alienated by material and spiritual poverty in all its forms. Together with the whole of creation, humanity experiences a profound nostalgia for a paradise lost, in which justice, wellbeing and peace prevail. The church's responsibility is to bring to this tormented and enslaved world the vigorous response of God to its questionings and rebellions. This response is the living truth of Christ which reaches down into the very depths of our being and liberates us. It is also the gift of the infinite love and compassion of God who ignores no human suffering and distress, and towards whom the blood and tears of the oppressed arise in mute appeal.

In every area of human activity there needs to be a constant reminder, in season and out of season, of the meaning of human dignity, of the unique and intrinsic value of the human person who cannot be reduced to a mere cog in the social machine. The church of Christ cannot shut its eyes to, or rest content with merely pious words about the deeply ingrained defects which disfigure modern society, nor ignore the inequalities in the distribution, use and management of the material riches of the earth of which human beings are meant to be the stewards. Nor can it be indifferent to the hunger and destitution of a large proportion of humankind. Is real solidarity still possible within the vast community of Christ's disciples, in the face of the ocean of suffering and poverty, especially in the third world, around us? We should not forget the social preaching of St. John Chrysostom who reminded the rich and powerful of his time (4th c.) that compassion to the poor is also a sacred liturgy in which human beings are the priests and which in God's sight has an incomparable dignity.

In speaking of poverty the church does not identify its message with the political and social programmes of our time. Yet the church cannot turn a blind eye to the fact of human poverty with which a great part of humanity is burdened today. Poverty and its consequences are themselves only the fruit of a deep disorder from which humanity has suffered since the fall of Adam. None of the social programmes and efforts to achieve prosperity and justice are able to bring humankind healing for the ills of sin, hatred, egotism, pride. It is when people become slaves of spiritual and physical passions that they succumb to poverty in a very real form, especially when they fail to realize it.

The Gospel of Liberation
The gospel of Christ is a message of life and healing addressed to all who are poor on this earth. From all, the gospel demands thorough conversion, the abandonment of human glory and the abjuring of the idols we have made of money, political and economic power, ideologies, etc. The gospel alone brings to all people, whatever their racial, social or political origin, true liberation and life.

This radical conversion of the heart is the principal fruit of the invisible action of the Holy Spirit within us, fashioning us in the image and likeness of him who though "he was rich, yet for your sake . . . became poor, so that by his poverty you might become rich" (II Cor. 8:9). The equality of brothers and sisters, and the freedom in the Spirit, experienced in the liturgy, should normally be expressed and continued in economic sharing and in liberation from social oppression. The disciples of Christ are called to a voluntary poverty that makes it possible for them, on the one hand, to become available for the inauguration of the kingdom of Christ in our human life and, on the other hand, to serve their own apprenticeship to love and complete sharing, and to communicate it to others.

A Therapy for the Sick World
This community that lives by the perennial liturgical *anamnesis* of creation and redemption bears witness to Jesus Christ through its daily liturgy of intercessory prayer for and loving service to the world. Orthodoxy, or the right glorification of God in eucharistic worship, results in orthopraxy or the life of prayer and service in the lives of individuals, groups, and congregations.

The therapy that the church experiences in the eucharist and in the other mysteries of the church should result in a therapy for the sick world. This does not mean a system of social ethics that the church prescribes for its members; it implies, rather, a healing ministry directed not only towards individuals in the world, but also towards its socio-economic and political life. The compassion of the church for the whole creation works itself out in the struggle against the world rulers of darkness, against injustice and oppression, against the denial of freedom and dignity for all, against torture and confinement without trial, against the suppression of minorities, against the violation of human rights. It results also in positive services to humanity, for education and health, for sane and healthy human communities, for just and equitable economic development, for a stable and strong family, and for making a human life possible for all.

The actual form and content of this *philanthropia* and *diakonia* will vary from country to country, from age to age. But in all times and all places the church has to be perceptive and sensitive as well as creative in suiting the *diakonia* to the needs of the people.

Orthopraxia
In different countries and societies there may exist different forms of service. In some cases the church's influence can extend to all aspects of society: social, economic, cultural, and political life. Each church is an agent of development in the context in which it lives and witnesses. In some situations, the church can be directly involved in the public and economic life of the nation. Thus, for example, in the middle east the local churches and the World Council of Churches are giving support to the suffering people of the region, providing financial assistance, building homes and hospitals for refugees, etc. In other contexts, the churches are able to serve the people by keeping homes for the aged, hospitals, educational institutions, etc. The church can and must contribute to the cultural life of the society. National churches can be greatly enriched, for instance, by different forms of ecclesiastical art such as church architecture, iconography, hymnography and church music.

It must be emphasized that the churches should continue to exert their constructive influence on the social, public and cultural life of nations. In such circumstances when Christians cannot have direct influence, individual Christians can be the voice of the church.

The churches have a special God-given duty to work for the realization of justice and peace, for the development of peoples and nations. The churches should be ready to defend human rights (freedom of conscience, freedom of speech, of belief) and condemn their violations.

One of the noble tasks of the church today is to work for the preservation of peace on earth. It is important to recognize that in its Christian sense, peace does not mean merely the absence of violence or open conflicts. It means peace within the heart of each human being, peace with neighbours, peace in society and in the whole creation. The foundation of this kind of peace is to be found in the reconciliation of humankind with Jesus Christ. It is important to recognize that Christians are not necessarily seeking peace at any price. Rather, they seek only that peace that is based on justice and on the realization of human rights. When conflicts arise, however, they are to be solved by peaceful means and not by violence.

For Orthodox Christians and for Orthodox mission today, it is essential that our faith be expressed in everyday life as "Orthopraxia." It is our duty to participate in all aspects of society, contributing to just development of life. It is very important to remember, however, that the salvation of human beings and that of the world is the ultimate mission of the church. All our development expresses in an incomplete way our striving towards the kingdom of God, which can never be fully realized in this world, but only in the eschaton, the age to come.

8. MONASTIC LIFE
AND RENEWAL IN MISSION

Identity of the Monastic Life

There is no definition of the monk that would be fundamentally different from that of a Christian. To be a true monk or true nun is also to be a true Christian. Monastic life, as Christian life in general, remains a mystery; it is a mode of existence in the communion of faith and the love of God. In Jesus Christ, however, many different ways and diverse *charismata* co-exist in the life of the church itself (I Cor. 12:4-31). The Orthodox Church has always encouraged such diversity.

The presence of a monk in the world can only be a paradox. He is a pilgrim (I Pet. 1:1; 2:11) who does not belong to this world, but nevertheless finds himself within it (II Cor. 5:6-7).

Whatever definition one advances for the monastic vocation, it is bound to be criticized. Monastic life is called an *askesis*, but it is not an automatic mechanism for ensuring the salvation of souls. Of course the monk or nun practises asceticism, one of the natural dynamisms of human nature; monastic life cannot however be reduced to asceticism.

The monastic vocation does not create another superior state within the church. On the contrary, the monk is inclined to confess always and anew that "Christ Jesus came into the world to save sinners. And I am the foremost of [them]" (I Tim. 1:15). The monk is a man of the gospel; this means that he is a human being who thirsts for salvation in the resurrected Christ. The roots of the life of a monk are in repentance and faith, in a perpetual *metanoia* wherein he lives the reality of the fall of human nature, as also the new reality of salvation in Christ, in which he participates as a living and active member. In faith and in humility, he lives this continuous *metanoia* as a renewal of the baptismal gift, as a "growth in God" (Col. 2:1a), a growth towards one, and only one, goal – the union with God in Christ.

In fact, the whole of Christian life is rooted in the grace of baptism. Even if its character as "responsible conversion" is not fully realized, the monk recovers the grace and the water of baptism in the tears of "sorrowful joy," as St. John Climacus says. It is a truly evangelical life of children of God, the life in Christ, life in the Spirit, life in the community of faith, in the community which seeks the realization of the love of Christ.

Vocation of the Monastic Community

What is the vocation of a monastic community in today's world as well as in the life of the church today? The monastic vocation has existed germinally in the life of the church from its very beginning; its current forms, however, have a historical origin and are rooted in particular cultures and traditions.

There have been periods in the history of several local churches when they have existed without an organized or powerful monastic group, even as the church has existed for long periods without ecumenical councils. Even a glance at the history of the church, however, is sufficient to convince us of one fact: the life and witness of the monastic communities have shaped the worship, the theology, the spirituality, and the pastoral and apostolic ministries of the church through the centuries. In accordance with its needs and possibilities, each local church developed diverse forms of monastic life, which it has integrated into its pastoral, missionary and spiritual work through the ages.

Each period of renewal in the spiritual life of the churches has been marked by a corresponding renewal in the life of the monastic communities. In the Orthodox churches, the renewal of spiritual life today should begin with a revitalization of our monastic communities, both of monks and nuns.

The Apostle Paul exhorts all Christians not to be conformed to the spirit of the age (Rom. 12:1-2). The vocation of each Christian is to refuse to be shaped by the patterns of this world, but rather to take responsibility for it, in order to transcend it and transfigure it by the renewal of the mind. The monastic community responds to this appeal for liberation from conformism and for inner transformation in a more disciplined, more communitarian and more radical manner.

At the heart of the monastic discipline is the sanctification of time and the renewal of the inner person by unceasing prayer. It is in concentrating upon God in prayer and in seeking at the same time to embrace creation in love and intercession, that the monastic community opens the channels for the Spirit of God to transform both the individual and the community from within. It also thus enables the monk to resist the pressures of the world that drive him to the pursuit of all sorts of vanities. Through his direct experience of the world, as also by his gift of discernment, the monk can also help to go beyond a superficial understanding of the world, and help Christians to have a contemplative attitude to history and the created order.

The discipline of prayer – all the way from the eucharistic liturgy through the canonical daily offices to the perpetual prayer and invocation of the name of Jesus – can undoubtedly also be practised by a layperson. But, in general, monastic life makes better provision for practicing the discipline. All vows and commitments – whether it be to chastity, poverty and obedience, to silence and solitude, or to fasting and self-denial – can only be ancillary to the principal task, the life of prayer, that is the foundation of all monastic life. As this central principle of prayer becomes rooted in faith and in love, all other things are added to it.

To Live in the Spirit of the Gospel

Some Christians live in affluent and secular societies. They are unable to find in them spiritual values with which they can regulate their lives. Sensing this secular vacuum, they look to the monasteries. Indeed, all the faithful can find spiritual good in the monastic life. Many young people, ignorant of Christian monasticism, have wandered away to follow various forms of non-Christian ascetic practices. These expressions of certain pseudo-mystical lifestyles often have religious bases, but they are also often foreign to the good news of Jesus Christ. Some who seek that "peace from above" confuse it with a quiet return to nature. By reaffirming, clarifying and setting forth the ancient Christian monastic ideals, the church can offer an authentic Christian lifestyle to those seeking peace and integrity of life.

The church, which is the body of Christ in the world, existing and acting in the present social context, is itself in need of the contributions of a strong monasticism. It needs to remind itself of this great treasure of witnessing. It is also through monasticism that the church will continue not only to live but also to grow, revitalize and perfect itself in the spirit of the gospel. Given this authentic, living example of the life of sacrifice and self-denial, as witnessed to by monastic communities, the church has a real and valid touch-stone by which to measure and re-align its actions.

In some areas of the world, the joy of living together in the Lord is absent from the community. The weight of individual effort is borne without the Christian expression of oneness in fellowship. This communal, unifying experience of sharing is well expressed in monastic communities as a sign for all.

The Witness of the Martyrs

The phenomenon of monasticism takes up again in the church the witness of the martyrs of the early centuries. By the principle of non-attachment and availability for God and one's fellow human beings, the monk or nun bears witness to the eschaton inside the church, and thus exercises a truly prophetic ministry, in showing forth the gospel's way of the kingdom. It is the radical faithfulness of the martyrs that assures that the gates of hell shall not prevail against the church.

On the other hand, by its insistence on renunciation of the world and on the eschatological dimension of history, the monastic community runs the risk of becoming an escapist movement that seeks to run away from the major problems which preoccupy the minds of other members of the church who live in society. It is the duty of the monk, as part of his task of spiritual direction, to help the faithful to fulfil their responsibilities in society in full liberty and with discernment.

9. MISSION TO ALL PEOPLES

Christ, creator and saviour, does not require of us a uniform act of confession, for he is the centre of the diversity of forms. Each people, each nation, each culture puts its own genius at the service of the church which preaches and confesses Christ for the sake of mutual enrichment and of the gathering of all people in a reconciled family. We personally encounter Christ in the eucharistic communion, but his creative presence extends to the whole cosmos and leads all of history towards fulfilment in him. The church has always been confronted with the culture of the countries and nations to which it preached the word of God. Today also, in view of the foregoing, the church should proclaim the gospel in such a way as to enable the new society with its new cultural traditions and needs to apprehend and accept the good news of Jesus Christ, to respond to it and not to remain indifferent to it.

In doing so, the church's preaching must remain faithful to the message of the word of God. It addresses the world through the mediation of human languages and cultures in order to transfigure it without conforming to it or alienating it. Through its presence the church gives a new dimension to the world.

In order to accomplish this task, the church should seek every opportunity to engage in and pursue the dialogue with the world, both within and without the ecclesial community, in order to prepare the "way of the Lord" (Matt. 3:3).

Finally, the dialogue with the world that "prepares the way of the Lord" will happen at the very place where the members of the eucharistic community live and work. It is they who are the true witness of the living Christ.

The Importance of the Cultural Milieu

The involvement of the whole person in the liturgical action presupposes that sanctification reaches not only each individual, but his or her entire environment. The reverse is also true; each Christian who actively participates in worship may bring into it his or her cultural heritage and personal creativity. This process presupposes a selection, based on Christian values. Not every cultural form found in our unredeemed world is qualified to serve as a meaningful liturgical expression. At all times, however, in the culture of various nations, the church has succeeded in finding and adopting cultural forms, which, through their richness and variety, were able to communicate the gospel to these peoples in a manner akin to their mentality and their historical traditions.

Through the liturgy, the Christian faith penetrates into the very depth of the life of the people. This presupposes that the language, the music, the icons, and the patterns of thought used in the liturgy be created by the communities which are deeply rooted both in the living tradition of the church and in the life of contemporary people. The marriage of Orthodox identity with local cultures in such a way that the latter be transfigured by the former is long and difficult:
– Foreign languages and forms of expressions used by ancient Orthodox people cannot be imposed upon indigenous Orthodox communities, yet neither can profane forms of expression of non-Orthodox people be indiscriminately introduced into the liturgy. Though new languages (Polish, Finnish, Hindi, French, English, etc.), new petitions in the litanies corresponding to new needs, new music, new vocabularies and patterns of thought must gradually be used, this creation is only possible insofar as the new communities simultaneously progress in the understanding of Orthodox tradition.
– The fact that Orthodoxy readily embraces the various national cultures and uses them as powerful tools of mission, does not mean that the unity of the church – a God-established mark of the body of Christ – can be sacrificed to values belonging to ethnic cultures (Col. 3:10-11; Gal. 3:28).
– Liturgical creation must never be accomplished at the expense of fidelity to authentic tradition. This fidelity implies the liberty necessary to a real incarnation of the faith in indigenous civilization, which nevertheless can only be integrated into the liturgy by converted hearts which transfigure the given culture.

Gospel and Local Cultures
Each people, each local society, has received from the creator special aptitudes and special gifts; throughout its

history it has developed a specific personality. It has also, alas, cultivated its particular idols and been marked by its own forms of sin. Therefore, when the gospel encounters a local society, this society is called to conversion; at the same time it is called to develop its true personality and to use its specific gifts towards the edification of the church of Christ. Thus a local culture is progressively re-created in Christ, when the word of God finds its local, concrete and incarnate expression. When the culture of a local church is in symphony with the culture of the other local churches, when it is listening to them and being listened to by them, then this local culture is an essential element of conciliar fellowship and a genuine expression of catholic faith.

We live in prophetic times where Christians are no longer a powerful majority that can impose their voice. Many of us live in post-Christian cultures in the west and the east. It is essential not to be suspicious of the cultural context in which we live, but on the contrary to be open and enter into contact with all people and be ready to proclaim the good news. We are living in the period of the formation of a new technological age and it is essential for Christians to participate in this formation, to act as the leaven in the dough. Our new powerlessness gives us the opportunity of seeking new entry points for the gospel.

Before bringing the gospel to people of other cultures, we must first carefully study their past and present cultural expressions. Part of a concrete ecumenical vision of Orthodoxy is the pastoral freedom of the local churches as well as the creative encounter between faith and indigenous cultures. In order to nurture this, we must offer the essential elements of our common Christian heritage to help those belonging to other cultures to absorb the vitality of this heritage and to become fully Christian. We must then be ready to encourage this new Christian community without hurry nor in a superficial way, to express itself within its own culture.

Contextualization of Mission
What elements in the context of our witness present new challenges to the mission of the Orthodox Church? Given the demands and problems posed by changing situations, how can the fellowship of the universal Orthodox Church strengthen the witness of Orthodox churches in particular local situations? As Orthodox, we are living in pluralistic

societies, in very different and complex situations. We feel the need for closer cooperation of all Orthodox churches in this common witness but we recognize that certain historical burdens and present realities make this very difficult and, at times, even impossible.

Orthodox Christianity today exists within at least five very different historical contexts. We have examined the specificity of these five contexts but recognize that they do not take into account all situations.

Each of these contexts gives rise to specific problems but also to great challenges and opportunities.

The Islamic context
Missionary work is very difficult within the present Islamic context and we should not encourage new major missionary enterprises in Islamic countries but strengthen and help the existing local churches, showing greater sensitivity towards the difficult situation of these churches. We must help these churches to keep their identity and to reinforce their teaching ministry to the younger generations. The form of witness in the Islamic context is often that of resistance shown by a true spiritual vitality, faithfulness to the gospel and witnessing in everyday life. Our Christian witness should not be a defence of our own interests against others, but we need to be strong enough spiritually and sufficiently educated to become a bridge in entering into dialogue with Muslims.

In dialogues between Christians and Muslims, the Orthodox have a special contribution to make because they have some elements in common with Muslims, e.g., they share a common eastern way of thinking. We must remember that Orthodox indigenous churches were present in the middle east from the very beginning of the history of the areas concerned. These Orthodox churches must be engaged in a continuing dialogue with Muslims for the sake of better understanding. While showing sensitivity towards Muslims, we must help others to be aware of the present realities in Islamic countries and of the precarious situation of Christian communities in these countries. Together the churches should make a common plea for the respect of human rights and religious freedom in all countries.

The socialist context
This context constitutes in itself a new missionary situation in the history of the Orthodox Church. It is essential, there-

fore, for the churches not only to reinforce their witness in all its traditional forms but also to live Orthodoxy in a new way. Here the liturgical life of the organized communities is a powerful witness. Every liturgy is a public proclamation and veneration of the gospel at the church frontiers. The liturgical fellowship, however, has the vocation to extend its testimony to all aspects of the society, avoiding a dis-incarnate piety. Hence one of the most essential and difficult tasks of the church in such a situation is to maintain its various commitments to the people struggling for social justice against economic oppression and poverty. The task of the church is not to protect an historical image but to meet the people where they are living with a deep sense of humility and responsibility.

In many respects, the experience of the churches living in this context becomes meaningful for all Orthodox. We have learned from them anew that the encounter between the revelation of God and human history is a cruciform encounter and that in the process of the transmission of the gospel there is both acceptance and rejection of it. To remain faithful to the gospel that challenges every culture and ideology is a permanent struggle. In this situation the churches need to have a particular evangelical concern for the proper values and ideology of the society. This is a new missionary challenge. What has the Orthodox tradition to say to these values and ideologies that are in our midst? The tradition should make possible a creative response by providing a legitimate encounter between the gospel and culture at each time and in each place. The best lesson we can learn from tradition is to live Orthodoxy in each time in a new way, even in controversial times.

The old churches in a secular context
Here, too, it is essential to revitalize the spiritual life by living and interpreting the holy tradition in a new way, carefully distinguishing this tradition from traditions limited to time and space. This will enable a proper dialogue with new secular socio-political forces that the church must take seriously. The different organs of spiritual life (i.e., the clergy, the lay theologians and laypeople, the monasteries and associations) must join forces in common witness.

The old churches have a prophetic responsibility to see the signs of the time, they must try to understand the challenges and new possibilities given by God. There is a need for finding a new language, a new attitude towards the transformation of the society. The churches still have the possibility of being heard, but too often they remain passive and do not participate actively in the new society. There is a need to revitalize the liturgical life and take into account the thirst for an authentic and meaningful Christian life and love.

The diaspora communities and emerging local communities in western secularized societies

The diaspora situation cannot be separated from the ecumenical context. In common witness with Catholics and Protestants the Orthodox have their own specific contribution to make in rediscovering certain apostolic values. There is a specific Orthodox attitude towards beauty, coherence and wholeness, a rediscovery of our true humanity when we are united with our Creator; and for all this there is a great thirst in the west. It is also a great responsibility of the Orthodox to be present with Catholics and Protestants in the mass media and in common service to the sick, the poor, the refugees, migrants, etc.

As the churches in the diaspora live in a new situation that gives them the freedom to express Orthodox faith and tradition in a creative way, these diaspora churches must also be aware of their responsibility towards their mother churches in discovering new forms of evangelization and mission. But in order to witness effectively, it is essential for the different Orthodox churches in the diaspora to render a common and undivided witness, and to overcome their present divisions on the local and universal level. There is a need to reflect on the role of laity and youth in the situation of the diaspora, and to encourage and strengthen all efforts towards a common witness by all Orthodox in the diaspora (such as the Orthodox fraternity in the west).

The churches in the diaspora should be more aware of their responsibility to witness to their Orthodox faith within the ecumenical context of the western world; within the context of their legitimate concern for preserving their national identity they should be primarily concerned for a common Orthodox witness.

The context of developing churches

There is need for greater solidarity among all Orthodox churches so that the developing churches of Asia and Africa can face their spiritual and economic problems and be ready to anticipate resistance in the coming storms of the political and social changes in these countries. Well studied projects are needed in order to fully develop the local economic resources (such as agricultural or other self-help enterprises) so that the church can provide for the needs of the community. Training programmes for all forms of ministry and leadership should be intensified so that the local church may become the full and authentic expression of Orthodoxy within its culture and in its own place.

Our churches must be sensitized to support this mission with all their resources (persons, experience, finances). The churches of the diaspora can give special help because of their own situation and because they are more open to new contexts and needs. Their languages (English and French) enable them to be active in Africa. This is an urgent situation for which we must all share responsibility.

Difficulties of External Mission
At this time in our history, most Orthodox churches find it very difficult to speak of foreign missions. It certainly is not a live option for many of the national Orthodox churches. Their duty remains primarily within the churches and the nations in which they find themselves. Yet, other Orthodox churches are to be challenged for having both the opportunity and the resources, and not responding to the charge to "make disciples of all nations" (Matt. 28:19). The same may be said in reference to inter-Orthodox assistance, especially to the newer Orthodox in Africa, Alaska and Asia.

The mission and witness of the Orthodox Church in the modern world has also been hampered by a weakening of the sense of unity between the local autocephalous Orthodox churches. There has been a tendency to lose the sense that unity and mission are inseparable, that the divine love and unity cannot be convincingly preached by those who do not adopt it as the standard for their own lives. Thus, especially in those countries where Orthodox communities have a relatively recent history (e.g. America, Western Europe, Australia), there are territorially overlapping jurisdictions and a tendency, by autocephalous churches, to be motivated in their policies and actions by nationalism, which belongs to the "fallen" world. The mission of the Orthodox Church and its witness to the world suffers greatly from these inconsistencies and conflicts. They must be urgently resolved by a common accord of all the Orthodox churches.

Thus, the difficult and thorny question of the renewal of foreign mission by the church cannot be met or solved by any one of the particular Orthodox churches. We cannot deny the goal. Yet a unified and organized Orthodox approach is needed, lest we harm and do disservice to our fellow Orthodox. It certainly is an important element in our understanding of our total mission in the world today, from an Orthodox perspective. Part of our mission is also to protect and preserve Orthodoxy where it is found today. An honest recognition of our limitations and existential restrictions is required as well.

There is also a serious lack of communication among the Orthodox churches. Some churches require urgent help. Some others are capable of providing such help. The missionary efforts remain isolated, and the Orthodox witness in the world is fragmented. The Orthodox church must enter into communication and take all necessary steps for mutual help.

10. HISTORY OF
ORTHODOX MISSIONS

The Traditional Approach to Mission
Throughout its history, the Orthodox Church was involved in missionary work, preaching the word of God among nations which had never heard it. In particular, there are two aspects characterizing the traditional Orthodox approach to mission that are relevant to our situation today.

Personal and communal witness
Orthodox missions have often succeeded when they were conducted not as an organized endeavour, planned and supported from abroad, but as a spontaneous and personal witness of Christian life, holiness and communion with divine life. Sometimes such a witness was made by laymen or -women (St. Frumentios in Ethiopia, St. Nina in Georgia). In other cases, monastic communities brought to non-Christian societies such authentic models of common life in Christ, prayers, toil and service, that their mere presence was sufficient to make the Christian message accepted and understood (the monasteries of northern Russia).

Indigenization
Whether systematically planned or spontaneously improvised, Orthodox missions were generally based on the attempt to make Scripture and liturgy immediately acceptable to the new Christians, by having them translated into their native tongue and by having a native clergy assume leadership in the "young churches." The greatest historical instance of this approach is that of Sts. Cyril and Methodius in their mission among the Slavs. Their example was followed up to modern times (St. Nicholas of Japan). In the examples mentioned above, however, indigenization was never seen as an end in itself; concern was also given to cultural continuity between the mother church and the daughter churches (liturgy, art, music, etc.) which preserved the sense of the universal unity of the church.

Orthodoxy is proud of its foreign missionary tradition that

has not been carried out in a spirit of colonialism, but rather with the intent of adapting the faith to the manners, language, traditions and life-styles of the people to whom it brings the gospel. Wherever Orthodoxy is now active in such mission it must retain and expand that method.

The Missionary Legacy of Sts. Cyril and Methodius

1. On the occasion of the 1100th anniversary of the death of St. Methodius, we paused to reflect on the life and work of this great Orthodox missionary saint, who together with his brother, St. Cyril, was responsible for bringing the message of the gospel to the Slavic peoples and nations. Chosen for this purpose by St. Photios, Patriarch of Constantinople, these brothers were sent to new frontiers, where their methods proved successful in planting the seeds of Orthodox Christianity.

a) Our reflection led us to wonder who among us is faithful today to the missionary legacy bequeathed to us by Sts. Cyril and Methodius? Which hierarch today is sending missionaries to new frontiers? Who among us has the courage and the missionary spirit to "go forth beyond his/her own borders? Who, within Orthodoxy today, is fulfilling the great commission of our Lord and Saviour Jesus Christ, to "go and make disciples of all nations" (Matt. 28:19)?

b) This going forth is not an option for Christians. It is an apostolic command, a duty that must be taken seriously by any church that claims catholicity and apostolicity, that proclaims Jesus Christ as Lord and Saviour and as light of the world.

c) Though Christianity exists on every continent of the earth, it must be admitted that the gospel is still unknown in vast regions of these continents, encompassing many nations. The Lord's command, therefore, is still unfulfilled and the example of Sts. Cyril and Methodius is still before us to give us the courage and inspiration to confront, as they did, new cultures, new people, new languages that have yet to be baptized and transfigured by the good news.

d) Wherever there is stagnation and decline within world Orthodoxy, one can discern a failure to be engaged in mission. Where there is life and light, there are no borders. The Spirit compels that these be shared with those who are under the power of sin and injustice, whether at home or far away in places unpenetrated by the light of the Lord.

e) Within our churches, many, both clergy and laity, men

and women, young and old, receive the call, the urging of the Spirit to "go forth," to be the prophets of our age, to earn the acclamations of the Orthodox Church as "equals to the Apostles." The church must seek out these people, provide them with training and unfettered support, and send them forth with prayers and blessings to provide the fermentation for new eucharistic communities. The possibilities for monastics, women and youth in the area of mission are vast and need special cultivation.

f) A dynamic vision of the extension of the church is required to enable those who are sent to move freely and courageously in the diverse lifestyles that will be encountered. As we begin to reach out to the unreached, history has shown that new light and life will be discovered within as well. The seemingly unsurmountable problems of our churches will diminish in importance and the faith of nominal members and the non-believers around us will be envigorated and renewed. The gospel demands both internal and external mission, home and overseas at the same time.

2. The Orthodox and apostolic tradition teaches us that when the word (Logos) of God was made flesh (John 1:1 ff), he assumed the whole of creation, in order to renew the fallen world and transform it into the kingdom of God. This cosmic dimension of the risen body of the incarnate Son implies that the object of mission is not only individual conversions, but the transfiguration of the entire society.

3. The place where the world becomes kingdom is the eucharistic assembly, where the whole creation, represented by the bread and the wine, is changed by the Holy Spirit into the body and blood of the risen Christ, into the kingdom of God. The eucharist itself, therefore, is a missionary event, the dynamic heart of the ecclesial community in which both men and women find their diaconal and missionary role.

4. This ecclesial character of mission means that the church is the place where an entire society and all its cultural values are transformed by the incarnate word of God. The church is present for all the people, not just "its own." The church must go out of itself in order to reach those outside. In doing this, the church must be prepared to recognize all that is good and positive in the world, be ready to receive and transfigure these elements wherever found, to support the struggle for authentic social justice and peace in the name of the gospel. At the same time, the church must

discern the evil of the world and redeem it, remaining "without spot or blemish."

5. Mission is neither primarily nor fundamentally a matter of sociology and statistics, since the church is the power of resurrection, the sacrament of the risen Christ who communicates to humanity and the whole of creation his own resurrection and glorification. The missionary vocation of the church is to induce in the world the process of transfiguration. Therefore, every church is called to be a *dynamic* missionary church. Coordinating their missionary efforts could contribute immensely to the emergence of new churches in new places in the world.

6. This development has to start from a reality of local possibilities, and we all have many skills developed already, many riches received from God. If we try to discover these potentials, we will see that we have many hidden treasures that help to build up these communities. We have to fight pessimism, the feeling of expecting miracles without cooperation with God. Therefore, it is necessary to develop all our skills that will bear fruits and especially the sense of sharing these skills with humility.

7. From the apostolic age and throughout the centuries women played a very important and vital role in the life and mission of the church. In view of this tradition it is important to help Orthodox to identify the *role* and *place* of women in mission, education, diakonia and ecumenism in the church. It is a need today to provide the possibility for dialogue between Orthodox women, an exchange of their experiences and to prepare them for ecumenical participation.

The role of women as deaconesses must be reexamined and recognized as a form of ministry – diakonia in the church as it was in some periods of development of Christianity.

8. Our Orthodox churches and our people are constantly confronted with situations in various areas of the world that require common witness and solutions. While recognizing the difficulty to overcome those theological differences and disputes of the past that made Eastern and Oriental Churches suffer for centuries, we believe that immediate cooperation of all Orthodox through common witness and mission around the world constitutes an essential way to rediscover their full and visible unity.

9. The Orthodox have a specific understanding and experience of the encounter between *gospel* and *culture* throughout the centuries. Therefore, their participation in

the gospel-culture debate is of extreme importance. Culture as spiritual and material creation of the whole people is part of the ecclesial reality. This issue has to be seen in the light of the effort to find new forms of mission and common witness in the midst of secularized societies. This is a long-term process, and it belongs to the nature of tradition as the permanent self-understanding of the church. The task of the church is to implement in every situation its authentic commitment to the people in the fields of cultural development, social justice and peace.

11. THE UNITY OF THE CHURCH AND THE UNITY OF CHURCHES

The Division of Christians: A Scandal and an Impediment to the United Witness of the Church

The Orthodox Church confesses its faith in the oneness of the church. Therefore there can be no churches (in the plural) except as manifestations of the one true church. The unity of the church does not mean creating a worldwide organization, often called structural unity. The one church cannot be created by putting all the local churches and individual denominations into one worldwide structure.

The unity of the church is the unity in Christ, by the Spirit, with the triune God. The church is Christ's body, and there is only one body, as there is one Christ and one Spirit. The church then is that great mystery in which Christ unites to himself all those whom God has chosen, by the Holy Spirit. This includes all those from Adam and Eve till our day, and we the Christians living today form but a segment of that whole reality that spans the ages and unites heaven and earth. Thus the unity of the church means being united with this great, mysterious transcendent reality. It is this church that manifests itself in its catholic fullness in each local church; the local church is not to be conceived of as part of some other reality called the universal church, which is sometimes understood as composed of local churches.

The unity of the church thus is not simply something we confess in the creed, but also experience in the local church, as the eucharistic community presided over by the bishop with his presbyters and deacons.

The promises and assurances in the discourse and prayer of Christ recorded in St John 13:31-17:26, including the promise that when the Spirit of truth comes "He . . . will guide you into all the truth" (16:13), were fulfilled at pentecost. Christ came in the Spirit and formed those who believed in him into his body, the church. Thus pentecost is both the birthday of the church, and the continuing experience in history of those who have since joined the communion of those illumined and glorified in Christ. It is

69

thus that the prayer of Christ for unity (John 17:11) was fulfilled and is being fulfilled, and all the truth is being revealed.

It is also a unity that is to be consummated and manifested when Christ appears in glory; devoid of all spots and blemishes, freed from sin, perfectly united to the head of the body, Christ, sharing in the life of the triune God "that they all may be one, even as we are one" (John 17:11). This unity in the triune God, with Christ in us and we in Christ, Christ in the Father and the Father in Christ by the Spirit, as an eschatological reality, is the standard and norm for the unity of the church today. This church that is the "fullness of Christ" cannot itself be judged by us, for Christ with his church is the judge of the world itself.

The fact that this God-given unity of the church is something assured by God himself does not, however mean that the Orthodox need not be concerned about the unity of all churches, for which the World Council of Churches is a privileged instrument. The division of Christians is a scandal and an impediment to the united witness of the church. A world hungering for life can be ministered to much more effectively if all churches were united; but that union of churches has to be based on their unity with the one church, the body of Christ. Our efforts for the unity of all churches should be based on the norm and standard of the God-given and eschatological unity of the one holy, catholic and apostolic church of Jesus Christ in the triune God, the church which we confess in the creed and experience in history.

It is also a warning to the Orthodox participants not to be pressured into any minimalist conceptions of Christian unity and therefore of "intercommunion." We all acknowledge the Lord Jesus Christ as our God and our Saviour, we are all committed to live for the glory of the triune God, Father, Son and Spirit. We all acknowledge the unique and primary authority of the holy scriptures as the word of God. This is the recognized basis of our collaboration in the life of the World Council of Churches. But the Orthodox do believe that they bring something essential to the richness of the ecumenical fellowship. We live by a faith and tradition which has been handed down to us from Christ and the apostles. We wish to keep this tradition open to criticism from other Christian brothers and sisters; we are willing to learn where we are ignorant; we want to change those things which are wrong or contrary to the authentic tradition. But we should not be asked or pressured to be unfaithful to that tradition on the basis of some argument which appears rational and scripture-based.

We have a common need to widen the basis of our ecumenical fellowship. We need to understand afresh the fundamentals of the unbroken tradition of the church to which the Orthodox seek to bear witness.

Such openness is difficult, painful, for all of us. It is beyond our feeble powers. But the moment we confess that it is beyond our power, the transcendent power of the Spirit will take hold of us and lead us where the Spirit will, i.e. nearer to our God-given unity in the triune God, Father, Son and Holy Spirit.

The Dialectic of Openness and Community
We have to be open both to the healing and saving power of God, and open to the world, so that Jesus Christ becomes the life of the world.

We have to be fully open to the world, experiencing its suffering and joy, in true Christian "com-passion" or co-experiencing. We take upon ourselves the pain and suffering of the world, as we identify ourselves with the world in true acts of self-giving love. As we live in this double openness to God and to the world, the powers of the kingdom operate in us and transform us.

Such openness to the world cannot be achieved by giving some money while closing our hearts. Com-passion with the world means understanding and respecting people different from us – different in race or class, sex or status, belief or unbelief, religion or language, habits and manners.

The eucharist is offered at all times and in all places, not just for the church, but also for and on behalf of the whole of creation. Openness towards the whole of humanity and to the whole of creation is the hallmark of an authentic eucharistic spirituality.

And yet, our eucharistic openness to the whole world does not imply that the eucharistic community loses its identity as the chosen and elect body of Christ. While the eucharistic community itself cuts through all barriers of class and race, of Jew and Gentile, of bond and free, the community has its own integrity, and the unbaptized (including catechumens) are not allowed to share in the eucharist. The eucharist is an act of the community incorporated into Christ by baptism and chrismation. The community opens its doors to the world when the word of God is proclaimed, but closes its doors before it enters the presence of the Almighty where Christ is seated at the right hand of God and where the eucharistic sacrifice is offered eternally by Christ the High Priest.

This dialectic of alternate closing and opening of the doors (of the church, but not of our hearts) is the central mystery of the church's identity and cannot be compromised. Because the table is the Lord's, it does not follow that anyone can indiscriminately partake of the body and blood of the Lord. The eucharist is for the community; the fruit of the eucharistic life is for the world. The eucharist is offered on behalf of the whole creation but only members of the body of Christ, incorporated into Christ by baptism and chrismation and living his or her life in Christ, can partake of the holy mysteries. None of us are worthy of such participation but God, in his infinite mercy, has made us partakers of the mystery of the eucharist.

Part II

1. ECUMENICAL CONVICTIONS ON MISSION AND EVANGELISM

In the ecumenical discussions and experience, churches with their diverse confessions and traditions and in their various expressions as parishes, monastic communities, religious orders, etc., have learned to recognize each other as participants in the one worldwide missionary movement. Thus, together, they can affirm an ecumenical perception of Christian mission expressed in the following convictions under which they covenant to work for the kingdom of God.

1. Conversion
The proclamation of the gospel includes an invitation to recognize and accept in a personal decision the saving lordship of Christ. It is the announcement of a personal encounter, mediated by the Holy Spirit, with the living Christ, receiving his forgiveness and making a personal acceptance of the call to discipleship and a life of service. God addresses himself specifically to each of his children, as well as to the whole human race. Each person is entitled to hear the good news. Many social forces today press for conformity and passivity. Masses of poor people have been deprived of their right to decide about their lives and the life of their society. While anonymity and marginalization seem to reduce the possibilities for personal decisions to a minimum, God as Father knows each one of his children and calls each of them to make a fundamental personal act of allegiance to him and his kingdom in the fellowship of his people.

While the basic experience of conversion is the same, the awareness of an encounter with God revealed in Christ, the concrete occasion of this experience and the actual shape of the same differs in terms of our personal situation. The

* Selections from *Mission and Evangelism: An Ecumenical Affirmation*. Available from the Commission on World Mission and Evangelism, printed in the *International Review of Mission*, Vol. LXXI, No. 284 (October 1982) and as a WCC Mission Series publication in study guide form.

calling is to specific changes, to renounce evidences of the domination of sin in our lives and to accept responsibilities in terms of God's love for our neighbour. John the Baptist said very specifically to the soldiers what they should do; Jesus did not hesitate to indicate to the young ruler that his wealth was the obstacle to his discipleship.

Conversion happens in the midst of our historical reality and incorporates the totality of our life, because God's love is concerned with that totality. Jesus' call is an invitation to follow him joyfully, to participate in his servant body, to share with him in the struggle to overcome sin, poverty and death.

The importance of this decision is highlighted by the fact that God himself through his Holy Spirit helps the acceptance of his offering of fellowship. The New Testament calls this a new birth (John 3:3). It is also called conversion, metanoia, total transformation of our attitudes and styles of life. Conversion as a dynamic and ongoing process "involves a turning *from* and a turning *to*. It always demands reconciliation, a new relationship both with God and with others. It involves leaving our old security behind (Matt. 16:24) and putting ourselves at risk in a life of faith."[1] It is "conversion from a life characterized by sin, separation from God, submission to evil and the unfulfilled potential of God's image, to a new life characterized by the forgiveness of sins, obedience to the commands of God, renewed fellowship with God in trinity, growth in the restoration of the divine image and the realization . . . of the love of Christ . . ."[2]

The call to conversion, as a call to repentance and obedience, should also be addressed to nations, groups and families. To proclaim the need to change from war to peace, from injustice to justice, from racism to solidarity, from hate to love is a witness rendered to Jesus Christ and to his kingdom. The prophets of the Old Testament addressed themselves constantly to the collective conscience of the people of Israel calling the rulers and the people to repentance and to renewal of the covenant.

Many of those who are attracted to Christ are put off by what they see in the life of the churches as well as in individual Christians. How many of the millions of people in the

---

[1] *Your Kingdom Come*, Geneva, WCC, 1980, p. 196.
[2] *Confessing Christ Today*, Reports of Groups at a Consultation of Orthodox Theologians, p. 8.

world who are not confessing Jesus Christ have rejected him because of what they saw in the lives of Christians! Thus the call to conversion should begin with the repentance of those who do the calling, who issue the invitation. Baptism in itself is a unique act, the covenant that Christians no longer belong to themselves but have been bought forever with the blood of Christ and belong to God. But the experience of baptism should be constantly re-enacted by daily dying with Christ to sin, to themselves and to the world and rising again with him into the servant body of Christ to become a blessing for the surrounding community.

The experience of conversion gives meaning to people in all stages of life, endurance to resist oppression, and assurance that even death has no final power over human life because God in Christ has already taken our life with him, a life that is "hidden with Christ in God" (Col. 3:3).

2. The Gospel to all Realms of Life

In the Bible, religious life was never limited to the temple or isolated from daily life (Hos. 6:4-6; Isa. 58:6-7). The teaching of Jesus on the kingdom of God is a clear reference to God's loving lordship over all human history. We cannot limit our witness to a supposedly private area of life. The lordship of Christ is to be proclaimed to all realms of life. In the great commission, Jesus said to his disciples: "All authority in heaven and on earth has been given to me. Go, therefore, and make disciples of all nations, baptizing them in the name of the Father and of the Son and of the Holy Spirit, teaching them to obey all that I have commanded you. And lo, I am with you always, to the close of the age" (Matt. 28:19-20). The good news of the kingdom is a challenge to the structures of society (Eph. 3:9-10; 6:12) as well as a call to individuals to repent. "If salvation from sin through divine forgiveness is to be truly and fully personal, it must express itself in the renewal of these relations and structures. Such renewal is not merely a consequence but an essential element of the conversion of whole human beings."[3]

"The evangelistic witness is directed towards all of the ktisis (creation) which groans and travails in search of adoption and redemption . . . The transfiguring power of the holy trinity is meant to reach into every nook and cranny of our

---

[3] *Breaking Barriers*, Geneva, WCC, 1976, p. 233.

national life . . . The evangelistic witness will also speak to the structures of this world; its economic, political, and societal institutions . . . We must re-learn the patristic lesson that the church is the mouth and voice of the poor and the oppressed in the presence of the powers that be. In our own way we must learn once again 'how to speak to the ear of the King', on the people's behalf . . . Christ was sent for no lesser purpose than bringing the world into the life of God."[4]

In the fulfilment of its vocation, the church is called to announce good news in Jesus Christ, forgiveness, hope, a new heaven and a new earth; to denounce powers and principalities, sin and injustice; to console the widows and orphans, healing, restoring the brokenhearted; and to celebrate life in the midst of death. In carrying out these tasks, churches may meet limitations, constraints, even persecution from prevailing powers which pretend to have final authority over the life and destiny of people.

In some countries there is pressure to limit religion to the private life of the believer – to assert that freedom to believe should be enough. The Christian faith challenges that assumption. The church claims the right and the duty to exist publicly – visibly – and to address itself openly to issues of human concern. "Confessing Christ today means that the Spirit makes us struggle with . . . sin and forgiveness, power and powerlessness, exploitation and misery, the universal search for identity, the widespread loss of Christian motivation, and the spiritual longings of those who have not heard Christ's name. It means that we are in communion with the prophets who announced God's will and promise for humankind and society, with the martyrs who sealed their confession with suffering and death, and also with the doubtful who can only whisper their confession of the Name."[5]

The realm of science and technology deserves particular attention today. The everyday life of most children, women and men, whether rich or poor, is affected by the avalanche of scientific discoveries. Pharmaceutical science has revolutionized sexual behaviour. Increasingly sophisticated computers solve problems in seconds for which formerly a whole lifetime was needed; at the same time they become a means of invading the privacy of millions of people. Nuclear

---

[4] *Confessing Christ Today*, pp. 10 and 3.
[5] *Breaking Barriers*, p. 48.

power threatens the survival of life on this planet, while at the same time it provides a new source of energy. Biological research stands at the awesome frontier of interference with the genetic code which could – for better or for worse – change the whole human species. Scientists are, therefore, seeking ethical guidance. Behind the questions as to right or wrong decisions and attitudes, however, there are ultimate theological questions: what is the meaning of human existence? the goal of history? the true reality within and beyond what can be tested and quantified empirically? The ethical questions arise out of a quest for a new worldview, a faith.

The biblical stories and ancient creeds do furnish precious insights for witnessing to the gospel in the scientific world. Can theologians, however, with these insights, help scientists achieve responsible action in genetic engineering or nuclear physics? It would hardly seem possible so long as the great communication gap between these two groups persists. Those directly involved in and affected by scientific research can best discern and explicate the insights of Christian faith in terms of specific ethical positions.

Christian witness will point towards Jesus Christ in whom real humanity is revealed and who is in God's wisdom the centre of all creation, the "head over all things" (Eph. 1:10; 22f). This witness will show the glory and the humility of human stewardship on this earth.

3. The Church and its Unity in God's Mission
To receive the message of the kingdom of God is to be incorporated into the body of Christ, the church, the author and sustainer of which is the Holy Spirit. The churches are to be a sign for the world. They are to intercede as he did, to serve as he did. Thus Christian mission is the action of the body of Christ in the history of humankind – a continuation of pentecost. Those who through conversion and baptism accept the gospel of Jesus partake in the life of the body of Christ and participate in an historical tradition. Sadly there are many betrayals of this high calling in the history of the churches. Many who are attracted to the vision of the kingdom find it difficult to be attracted to the concrete reality of the church. They are invited to join in a continual process of renewal of the churches. "The challenge facing the churches is not that the modern world is unconcerned about their evangelistic message, but rather whether they are so renewed in their life and thought that they become a living witness

to the integrity of the gospel. The evangelizing churches need themselves to receive the good news and to let the Holy Spirit remake their life when and how he wills."[6]

The celebration of the eucharist is the place for the renewal of the missionary conviction at the heart of every congregation. According to the Apostle Paul, the celebration of the eucharist is in itself a "proclamation of the death of the Lord until he comes" (I Cor. 11:26). "In such ways God feeds his people as they celebrate the mystery of the eucharist so that they may confess in word and deed that Jesus Christ is Lord, to the glory of God the Father."[7]

The eucharist is bread for a missionary people. We acknowledge with deep sorrow the fact that Christians do not join together at the Lord's table. This contradicts God's will and impoverishes the body of Christ. The credibility of our Christian witness is at stake.

Christians are called to work for the renewal and transformation of the churches. Today there are many signs of the work of the Holy Spirit in such a renewal. The house gatherings of the church in China or the Basic Ecclesial Communities in Latin America, the liturgical renewal, biblical renewal, the revival of the monastic vocation, the charismatic movement, are indications of the renewal possibilities of the church of Jesus Christ.

In the announcement to the world of the reconciliation in Jesus Christ, churches are called to unite. Faced with the challenge and threat of the world, the churches often unite to defend common positions. But common witness should be the natural consequence of their unity with Christ in his mission. The ecumenical experience has discovered the reality of a deep spiritual unity. The common recognition of the authority of the Bible and of the creeds of the ancient church and a growing convergence in doctrinal affirmations should allow the churches not only to affirm together the fundamentals of the Christian faith, but also to proclaim together the good news of Jesus Christ to the world. In solidarity, churches are helping each other in their respective witness before the world. In the same solidarity, they should share their spiritual and material resources to announce together and clearly their common hope and common calling.

---

[6] Philip Potter's speech to the Roman Catholic Synod of Bishops, Rome, 1974.
[7] *Your Kingdom Come*, p. 206.

"Often it is socially and politically more difficult to witness together since the powers of this world promote division. In such situations common witness is particularly precious and Christ-like. Witness that dares to be common is a powerful sign of unity coming directly and visibly from Christ and a glimpse of his kingdom."[8]

The impulse for common witness comes from the depth of our faith. "Its urgency is underlined when we realize the seriousness of the human predicament and the tremendous task waiting for the churches at present."[9]

It is at the heart of Christian mission to foster the multiplication of local congregations in every human community. The planting of the seed of the gospel will bring forward a people gathered around the word and sacraments and called to announce God's revealed purpose.

Thanks to the faithful witness of disciples through the ages, churches have sprung up in practically every country. This task of sowing the seed needs to be continued until there is, in every human community, a cell of the kingdom, a church confessing Jesus Christ and in his name serving his people. A vital instrument for the fulfilment of the missionary vocation of the church is the local congregation.

The planting of the church in different cultures demands a positive attitude towards inculturation of the gospel. Ancient churches, through centuries of intimate relations with the cultures and aspirations of their people, have proved the powerful witnessing character of this rooting of the churches in the national soil. "Inculturation has its source and inspiration in the mystery of the incarnation. The word was made flesh. Here flesh means the fully concrete, human and created reality that Jesus was. Inculturation, therefore, becomes another way of describing Christian mission. If proclamation sees mission in the perspective of the word to be proclaimed, inculturation sees mission in the perspective of the flesh, or concrete embodiment, which the word assumes in a particular individual, community, institution or culture."[10]

Inculturation should not be understood merely as intellectual research; it occurs when Christians express their faith in the symbols and images of their respective culture. The

---

[8] *Common Witness*, p. 28.
[9] Ibid.
[10] SEDOS Bulletin 81/No. 7.

best way to stimulate the process of inculturation is to participate in the struggle of the less privileged for their liberation. Solidarity is the best teacher of common cultural values.

This growing cultural diversity could create some difficulties. In our attempt to express the catholicity of the church we may lose the sense of its unity. But the unity we look for is not uniformity but the multiple expression of a common faith and a common mission.

"We have found this confession of Christ out of our various cultural contexts to be not only a mutually inspiring, but also a mutually corrective exchange. Without this sharing our individual affirmations would gradually become poorer and narrower. We need each other to regain the lost dimensions of confessing Christ and to discover dimensions unknown to us before. Sharing in this way, we are all changed and our cultures are transformed."[11]

The vision of nations coming from the east, the west, the north and the south to sit at the final banquet of the kingdom should always be before us in our missionary endeavour.

4. Mission in Christ's Way

"As the Father has sent me, even so I send you" (John 20:21). The self-emptying of the servant who lived among the people, sharing in their hopes and sufferings, giving his life on the cross for all humanity – this was Christ's way of proclaiming the good news, and as disciples we are summoned to follow the same way. "A servant is not greater than his master; nor is he who is sent greater than he who sent him" (John 13:16).

Our obedience in mission should be patterned on the ministry and teaching of Jesus. He gave his love and his time to all people. He praised the widow who gave her last coin to the temple; he received Nicodemus during the night; he called Matthew to the apostolate; he visited Zacchaeus in his home; he gave himself in a special way to the poor, consoling, affirming and challenging them. He spent long hours in prayer and lived in dependence on and willing obedience to God's will.

An imperialistic crusader's spirit was foreign to him. Churches are free to choose the ways they consider best to announce the gospel to different people in different circumstances. But these options are never neutral. Every method-

---

[11] *Breaking Barriers*, p. 46.

ology illustrates or betrays the gospel we announce. In all communications of the gospel, power must be subordinate to love.

Our societies are undergoing a significant and rapid change under the impact of new communication technologies and their applications. We are entering the age of the information society, characterized by an ever-increasing media presence in all relationships, both interpersonal and intersocial. Christians need to re-think critically their responsibility for all communication processes and re-define the values of Christian communications. In the use of all new media options, the communicating church must ensure that these instruments of communication are not masters, but servants in the proclaiming of the kingdom of God and its values. As servants, the new media options, kept within their own limits, will help to liberate societies from communication bondage and will place tools in the hands of communities for witnessing to Jesus Christ.

Evangelism happens in terms of interpersonal relations when the Holy Spirit quickens to faith. Through sharing the pains and joys of life, identifying with people, the gospel is understood and communicated.

Often, the primary confessors are precisely the non-publicized, unsensational people who gather together steadfastly in small caring communities, whose life prompts the question: "What is the source of the meaning of your life? What is the power of your powerlessness?", giving the occasion to name *the name*. Shared experiences reveal how often Christ is confessed in the very silence of a prison cell or of a restricted but serving, waiting, praying church.

Mission calls for a serving church in every land, a church which is willing to be marked with the stigmata (nailmarks) of the crucified and risen Lord. In this way the church will show that it belongs to that movement of God's love shown in Christ who went to the periphery of life. Dying outside the gates of the city (Heb. 13:12) he is the high priest offering himself for the salvation of the world. Outside the city gates the message of a self-giving, sharing love is truly proclaimed, here the church renews its vocation to be the body of Christ in joyful fellowship with its risen Lord (I John 3:16).

5. Good News to the Poor

There is a new awareness of the growing gap between wealth and poverty among the nations and inside each nation. It is a cruel reality that the number of people who do not reach the material level for a normal human life is growing steadily. An increasing number of people find themselves marginalized, second-class citizens unable to control their own destiny and unable to understand what is happening around them. Racism, powerlessness, solitude, breaking of family and community ties are new evidences of the marginalization that comes under the category of poverty.

There is also a tragic coincidence that most of the world's poor have not heard the good news of the gospel of Jesus Christ; or they could not receive it, because it was not recognized as good news in the way in which it was brought. This is a double injustice: they are victims of the oppression of an unjust economic order or an unjust political distribution of power, and at the same time they are deprived of the knowledge of God's special care for them. To announce the good news to the poor is to begin to render the justice due to them. The church of Jesus Christ is called to preach the good news to the poor following the example of its Lord who was incarnated as poor, who lived as one among them and gave to them the promise of the kingdom of God. Jesus looked at the multitudes with compassion. He recognized the poor as those who were sinned against, victims of both personal and structural sin.

Out of this deep awareness came both his solidarity and his calling to them (Matt. 11:28). His calling was a personalized one. He invited them to come to him, to receive forgiveness of sins and to assume a task. He called them to follow him, because his love incorporated his respect for them as people created by God with freedom to respond. He called them to exercise this responsibility towards God, neighbours and their own lives. The proclamation of the gospel among the poor is a sign of the messianic kingdom and a priority criterion by which to judge the validity of our missionary engagement today.

This new awareness is an invitation to re-think priorities and lifestyles both in the local church and in the worldwide missionary endeavour. Of course, churches and Christians find themselves in very different contexts: some in very wealthy settings where the experience of poverty as it is known to millions in the world today is practically unknown, or in egalitarian societies of extreme poverty. But the consciousness of the global nature of poverty and exploitation in the world today, the knowledge of the interdependence between nations and the understanding of the international missionary responsibility of the church – all invite, in fact oblige, every church and every Christian to think of ways and means to share the good news with the poor of today. An objective look at the life of every society, even the most affluent and those which are, theoretically, more just, will show the reality of the poor today in the marginalized, the drop-outs who cannot cope with modern society, the prisoners of conscience, the dissidents. All of them are waiting for a cup of cold water or for a visit in the name of Christ. Churches are learning afresh through the poor of the earth to overcome the old dichotomies between evangelism and social action. The "spiritual gospel" and "material gospel" were in Jesus one gospel.

There is no evangelism without solidarity; there is no Christian solidarity that does not involve sharing the knowledge of the kingdom which is God's promise to the poor of the earth. There is here a double credibility test: A proclamation that does not hold forth the promises of the justice of the kingdom to the poor of the earth is a caricature of the gospel; but Christian participation in the struggles for justice which does not point towards the promises of the kingdom also makes a caricature of a Christian understanding of justice.

A growing consensus among Christians today speaks of God's preferential option for the poor.[12] We have there a valid yardstick to apply to our lives as individual Christians, local congregations and as missionary people of God in the world.

This concentration point, God's preferential option for the poor, raises the question of the gospel for all those who objectively are not poor or do not consider themselves as such. It is a clear Christian conviction that God wants all human beings to be saved and to come to the knowledge of truth, but we know that, while God's purpose is for the salvation of all, he has worked historically through the people of Israel and through the incarnation of his own son Jesus Christ. While his purpose is universal, his action is always particular. What we are learning anew today is that God works through the downtrodden, the persecuted, the poor of the earth. And from there, he is calling all humanity to follow him. "If any one would come after me, let him

---

[12] Catholic Bishops Conference, Puebla, 1979, para. 1134.

deny himself and take up his cross and follow me" (Matt. 16:24).

For all of us, the invitation is clear: to follow Jesus in identification and sharing with the weak, marginalized and poor of the world, because in them we encounter him. Knowing from the gospel and from historical experience that to be rich is to risk forfeiting the kingdom, and knowing how close the links are, in today's world, between the abundance of some and the needs of others, Christians are challenged to follow him, surrendering all they are and have to the kingdom, to a struggle that commits us against all injustice, against all want. The preferential option for the poor, instead of discriminating against all other human beings, is, on the contrary, a guideline for the priorities and behaviour of all Christians everywhere, pointing to the values around which we should organize our lives and the struggle in which we should put our energy.

There is a long experience in the church of voluntary poverty, people who in obedience to their Christian calling cast aside all their belongings, make their own the fate of the poor of the earth, becoming one of them and living among them. Voluntary poverty has always been recognized as a source of spiritual inspiration, of insight into the heart of the gospel.

Today we are gratefully surprised, as churches are growing among the poor of the earth, by the insight and perspective of the gospel coming from the communities of the poor. They are discovering dimensions of the gospel which have long been forgotten by the church. The poor of the earth are reading reality from the other side, from the side of those who do not get the attention of the history books written by the conquerors, but who surely get God's attention in the book of life. Living with the poor and understanding the Bible from their perspective helps to discover the particular caring with which God both in the Old and in the New Testament thinks of the marginalized, the downtrodden and the deprived. We realize that the poor to whom Jesus promised the kingdom of God are blessed in their longing for justice and in their hope for liberation. They are both subjects and bearers of the good news; they have the right and the duty to announce the gospel not only among themselves, but also to all other sectors of the human family.

Churches of the poor are spreading the liberating gospel of Jesus Christ in almost every corner of the earth. The richness and freshness of their experience is an inspiration and blessing to churches with a centuries-old history. The centres of the missionary expansion of the church are moving from the north to the south. God is working through the poor of the earth to awaken the consciousness of humanity to his call for repentance, for justice and for love.

6. Mission in and to Six Continents
Everywhere the churches are in missionary situations. Even in countries where the churches have been active for centuries we see life organized today without reference to Christian values, a growth of secularism understood as the absence of any final meaning. The churches have lost vital contact with the workers and the youth and many others. This situation is so urgent that it commands priority attention of the ecumenical movement. The movement of migrants and political refugees brings the missionary frontier to the doorstep of every parish. The Christian affirmations on the worldwide missionary responsibility of the church will be credible if they are authenticated by a serious missionary engagement at home.

As the world becomes smaller, it is possible even for Christians living far away to be aware of and inspired by faithful missionary engagement in a local situation. Of special importance today is the expression of solidarity among the churches crossing political frontiers and the symbolic actions of obedience of one part of the body of Christ that enhance the missionary work of other sectors of the church. So, for example, while programmes related to the elimination of racism may be seen as problems for some churches, such programmes have become, for other churches, a sign of solidarity, an opportunity for witness and a test of Christian authenticity.

Every local congregation needs the awareness of its catholicity which comes from its participation in the mission of the church of Jesus Christ in other parts of the world. Through its witnessing stance in its own situation, its prayers of intercession for churches in other parts of the world, and its sharing of persons and resources, it participates fully in the world mission of the Christian church.

This concern for mission everywhere has been tested with the call for a moratorium, a halt – at least for a time – to sending and receiving missionaries and resources across national boundaries, in order to encourage the recovery and affirmation of the identity of every church, the concentration on mission in its own place and the freedom to reconsider traditional relations. The Lausanne Covenant noted that "the reduction of foreign missionaries and money in an evangelized country may sometimes be necessary to facilitate the national church's growth and self-reliance and to release resources for unevangelized areas."[13] Moratorium does not mean the end of the missionary vocation nor of the duty to provide resources for missionary work, but it does mean freedom to reconsider present engagements and to see whether a continuation of what we have been doing for so long is the right style of mission in our day.

Moratorium has to be understood inside a concern for world mission. It is faithfulness of commitment to Christ in each national situation which makes missionary concern in other parts of the world authentic. There can never be a moratorium of mission, but it will always be possible, and sometimes necessary, to have a moratorium for the sake of better mission.

The story of the churches from their earliest years is the story of faithfulness in their respective localities, but also the story of the carrying of the gospel across national and continental boundaries; first from Jerusalem to Judaea and Samaria, then to Asia Minor, Africa and Europe, now to the ends of the earth. Christians today are the heirs of a long history of those who left their home countries and churches, apostles, monastics, pilgrims, missionaries, emigrants, to work in the name of Jesus Christ, serving and preaching where the gospel had not yet been heard or received. With the European colonization of most of the world and later on with the expansion of the colonial and neo-colonial presence of the western powers, the churches which had their bases mainly in the west have expanded their missionary service to all corners of the earth.

Surely, many ambiguities have accompanied this development and are present even today, not least the sin of proselytism among other Christian confessions. Churches and missionary organizations are analysing the experience of these past centuries in order to correct their ways, precisely with the help of the new churches which have come into being in those countries. The history of the church, the missionary people of God, needs to continue. Each local

---

[13] Lausanne Covenant, No. 9.

parish, each Christian, must be challenged to assume responsibility in the total mission of the church. There will always be need for those who have the calling and the gift to cross frontiers, to share the gospel of Jesus Christ and to serve in his name.

Out of this sense of being the whole church in mission, we recognize the specific calling to individuals or communities to commit themselves full time to the service of the church, crossing cultural and national frontiers. The churches should not allow this specialized calling of the few to be an alibi for the whole church, but rather it should be a symbolic concentration of the missionary vocation of the whole church. Looking at the question of people in mission today, "We perceive a change in the direction of mission, arising from our understanding of the Christ who is the centre and who is always in movement towards the periphery. While not in any way denying the continuing significance and necessity of a mutuality between the churches in the northern and southern hemispheres, we believe that we can discern a development whereby mission in the eighties may increasingly take place within these zones. We feel there will be increasing traffic between the churches of Asia, Africa and Latin America among whose numbers both rich and poor are counted. This development, we expect, will take the form of ever stronger initiatives from the churches of the poor and oppressed at the peripheries. Similarly among the industrialized countries, a new reciprocity, particularly one stemming from the marginalized groups, may lead to sharing at the peripheries of the richer societies. While resources may still flow from financially richer to poorer churches, and while it is not our intention to encourage isolationism, we feel that a benefit of this new reality could well be the loosening of the bond of domination and dependence that still so scandalously characterizes the relationship between many churches of the northern and southern hemispheres respectively."[14]

7. Witness among People of Living Faiths
Christians owe the message of God's salvation in Jesus Christ to every person and to every people. Christians make their witness in the context of neighbours who live by other religious convictions and ideological persuasions. True

---

[14] *Your Kingdom Come*, pp. 220/221.

witness follows Jesus Christ in respecting and affirming the uniqueness and freedom of others. We confess as Christians that we have often looked for the worst in others and have passed negative judgement upon other religions. We hope as Christians to be learning to witness to our neighbours in a humble, repentant and joyful spirit.

The word is at work in every human life. In Jesus of Nazareth the word became a human being. The wonder of his ministry of love persuades Christians to testify to people of every religious and non-religious persuasion of this decisive presence of God in Christ. In him is our salvation. Among Christians there are still differences of understanding as to how this salvation in Christ is available to people of diverse religious persuasions. But all agree that witness should be rendered to all.

Such an attitude springs from the assurance that God is the creator of the whole universe and that he has not left himself without witness at any time or any place. The Spirit of God is constantly at work in ways that pass human understanding and in places that to us are least expected. In entering into a relationship of dialogue with others, therefore, Christians seek to discern the unsearchable riches of God and the way he deals with humanity. For Christians who come from cultures shaped by another faith, an even more intimate interior dialogue takes place as they seek to establish the connection in their lives between their cultural heritage and the deep convictions of their Christian faith.

Christians should use every opportunity to join hands with their neighbours, to work together to be communities of freedom, peace and mutual respect. In some places, state legislation hinders the freedom of conscience and the real exercise of religious freedom. Christian churches as well as communities of other faiths cannot be faithful to their vocation without the freedom and right to maintain their institutional form and confessional identity in a society and to transmit their faith from one generation to another. In those difficult situations, Christians should find a way, along with others, to enter into dialogue with the civil authorities in order to reach a common definition of religious freedom. With that freedom comes the responsibility to defend through common actions all human rights in those societies.

Life with people of other faiths and ideologies is an encounter of commitments. Witness cannot be a one-way process, but of necessity is two-way; in it Christians become aware of some of the deepest convictions of their neighbours. It is also the time in which, within a spirit of openness and trust, Christians are able to bear authentic witness, giving an account of their commitment to the Christ, who calls all persons to himself.

2. THE EUCHARIST: BREAD AND WINE FOR PILGRIMS ON THEIR APOSTOLIC JOURNEY

The Eucharist as Communion of the Faithful

The eucharistic communion with Christ who nourishes the life of the church is at the same time communion within the body of Christ which is the church. The sharing in one bread and the common cup in a given place demonstrates and effects the oneness of the sharers with Christ and with their fellow sharers in all times and places. It is in the eucharist that the community of God's people is fully manifested. Eucharistic celebrations always have to do with the whole church, and the whole church is involved in each local eucharistic celebration. In so far as a church claims to be a manifestation of the whole church, it will take care to order its own life in ways which take seriously the interests and concerns of other churches.

The eucharist embraces all aspects of life. It is a representative act of thanksgiving and offering on behalf of the whole world. The eucharistic celebration demands reconciliation and sharing among all those regarded as brothers and sisters in the one family of God and is a constant challenge in the search for appropriate relationships in social, economic and political life (Matt. 5:23f; I Cor. 10:16f; I Cor. 11:20-22; Gal. 3:28). All kinds of injustice, racism, separation and lack of freedom are radically challenged when we share in the body and blood of Christ. Through the eucharist the all-renewing grace of God penetrates and restores human personality and dignity. The eucharist involves the believer in the central event of the world's history. As participants in the eucharist, therefore, we prove inconsistent if we are not actively participating in this ongoing restoration of the world's situation and the human condition. The eucharist shows us that our behaviour is inconsistent in face of the reconciling presence of God in human history: we are placed under continual judgment by the persistence of unjust

---

* Selection from Faith and Order Paper 111 on Baptism, Eucharist and Ministry, published by the World Council of Churches.

relationships of all kinds in our society, the manifold divisions on account of human pride, material interest and power politics and, above all, the obstinacy of unjustifiable confessional oppositions within the body of Christ.

Solidarity in the eucharistic communion of the body of Christ and responsible care of Christians for one another and the world find specific expression in the liturgies: in the mutual forgiveness of sins; the sign of peace; intercession for all; the eating and drinking together; the taking of the elements to the sick and those in prison or the celebration of the eucharist with them. All these manifestations of love in the eucharist are directly related to Christ's own testimony as a servant, in whose servanthood Christians themselves participate. As God in Christ has entered into the human situation, so eucharistic liturgy is near to the concrete and particular situations of men and women. In the early church the ministry of deacons and deaconesses gave expression in a special way to this aspect of the eucharist. The place of such ministry between the table and the needy properly testifies to the redeeming presence of Christ in the world.

The Eucharist as Meal of the Kingdom

The eucharist opens up the vision of the divine rule which has been promised as the final renewal of creation, and is a foretaste of it. Signs of this renewal are present in the world wherever the grace of God is manifest and human beings work for justice, love and peace. The eucharist is the feast at which the church gives thanks to God for these signs and joyfully celebrates and anticipates the coming of the kingdom in Christ (I Cor. 11:26; Matt. 26:29).

The world, to which renewal is promised, is present in the whole eucharistic celebration. The world is present in the thanksgiving to the Father, where the church speaks on behalf of the whole creation; in the memorial of Christ, where the church, united with its great High Priest and Intercessor, prays for the world; in the prayer for the gift of the Holy Spirit, where the church asks for sanctification and new creation.

Reconciled in the eucharist, the members of the body of Christ are called to be servants of reconciliation among men and women and witnesses of the joy of resurrection. As Jesus went out to publicans and sinners and had table-fellowship with them during his earthly ministry, so Christians are called in the eucharist to be in solidarity with the outcast and to become signs of the love of Christ who lived and sacrificed himself for all and now gives himself in the eucharist.

The very celebration of the eucharist is an instance of the church's participation in God's mission to the world. This participation takes everyday form in the proclamation of the gospel, service of the neighbour, and faithful presence in the world.

As it is entirely the gift of God, the eucharist brings into the present age a new reality which transforms Christians into the image of Christ and therefore makes them his effective witnesses. The eucharist is precious food for missionaries, bread and wine for pilgrims on their apostolic journey. The eucharistic community is nourished and strengthened for confessing by word and action the Lord Jesus Christ who gave his life for the salvation of the world. As it becomes one people, sharing the meal of the one Lord, the eucharistic assembly must be concerned for gathering also those who are at present beyond its visible limits, because Christ invited to his feast all for whom he died. Insofar as Christians cannot unite in full fellowship around the same table to eat the same loaf and drink from the same cup, their missionary witness is weakened at both the individual and the corporate levels.

3. CHRISTIAN WITNESS
– COMMON WITNESS

The Common Ground

The command of Jesus Christ and the power of his grace leads the church to proclaim the good news he has brought us; finally this good news is Christ himself. This gospel message gives Christian communities the common ground for their proclamation. They accept the content of the biblical witness and the creeds of the early church. Today they desire to reach beyond what separates them by stressing the essential and returning to the foundation of their faith, Jesus Christ (I Cor. 3:11), (cf. *Common Witness and Proselytism*, 2). They recognize that baptism, as the effective sign of their unity, brings them into communion with Christ's followers and empowers them to confess him as Lord and Saviour. Therefore the Lord's gift of unity already exists among Christians and, although it is not yet realized perfectly, it is real and operative. This unmerited gift requires that witness be borne in common as an act of gratitude and the witness in turn is a means of expressing and deepening unity.

The Source of Witness

The Father

Christian witness has its source in the Father who testified to Christ his beloved Son, sent visibly into the world; he bore witness to him on the cross and by raising him from the dead through the Holy Spirit. So Christ received the fulness of the Holy Spirit to be in the world, himself the divine fulness for the human family (Col. 2:9-10).

"When God raised up his servant, he sent him to bless you" (Acts 3:26; 26:23). Jesus could say: "I am going away and I shall come back to you" (John 14:28). He who "has

---

* Selections from *Common Witness*, a study document of the Joint Working Group of the Roman Catholic Church and the World Council of Churches, published by the WCC.

become for us wisdom and justification, sanctification and liberation" (I Cor. 1:30) has been sent into the world that those who receive him in faith may find in him that sanctification and liberation. God now sends him into the world in the church which he has made his body in spite of the sin of its members. The disciple can say: "Christ lives in me" (Gal. 2:20; cf. II Cor. 4:10-12) and "Christ speaks in me" (II Cor. 13:3). Christian witness is an epiphany of Christ who took the form of a servant and became obedient unto death (Phil. 2:6).

Jesus Christ

Jesus Christ is the one witness of God, true and faithful (Rev. 3:14; 1:5; vid. *Confessing Christ Today*: 8, 9, 10). The witness he gave to the Father through his life was sealed by the martyrdom of the cross. His death evidenced total dedication to the witness he bore; it was the testimony he gave to himself as "the truth that liberates" (John 8:32). The cause of the Father had consumed his life to the point of martyrdom. In his death and resurrection his entire existence disclosed the meaning of the message. Through those events he breathed forth his Spirit to animate his followers, drawing them together in the community of witness, his mystical body which is the church. It would pay a similar price for the witness which he would give through it (I Pet. 5:9). From the beginning the followers of Jesus as confessors and martyrs became the vehicle of the Spirit in their suffering unto death, inseparably linked with the inspired words they uttered in the power of the same Spirit.

The Holy Spirit

The Spirit plays such an important role in Christian witness that he too can be said to be the witness of Christ in the world: "The Spirit of truth himself who comes from the Father will bear witness to me" (John 15:26). For it is in the Spirit that God raises Christ (Rom. 8:11); it is in the Spirit that he glorifies him (John 16:14-15); it is the Spirit who convicts the world in the trial which brings it into contradiction with Jesus (John 16:8). The Spirit bears this witness by means of the church. He makes the church the body (I Cor. 12:13) and thus the manifestation of Christ in this world. The Spirit is communion (II Cor. 13:13) so he unites us to Christ; and in the same movement, brings about communion among men and women.

The Spirit comes upon the faithful and makes them also witnesses of Christ (Acts 1:8). In him the word and action of Christians becomes a "demonstration of spirit and power" (I Cor. 2:4). We must encounter Christ to be his witnesses, to be able to say what we know about him (cf. I John 1:3-4; 4:14). It is the Holy Spirit who enables the faithful to meet Christ, to experience him. Believers are led to witness to their faith before humankind, because the Spirit witnesses to Jesus in their hearts (John 15:16-17; Rom. 8:16; Gal. 4:6). In the debate between Jesus and the world, he takes the part of Jesus in strengthening believers in their faith (John 16:8; cf. I John 5, 6), but he also deepens the faith of believers by leading them to the whole truth (John 16:13). He is thus the master of Christian witness enabling us to say "Jesus is Lord" (I Cor. 12:3), he is the inspiration and teacher of the church (John 16:13).

The Church
The church received its commission from the Lord Jesus Christ himself, "You shall be my witnesses" (Acts 1:8). It takes upon itself the witness which the Father bore to his Son (cf. John 5:32) when, in front of those who put him to death, he raised him and made him Christ and Lord for the salvation of all (Acts 2:23, 24, 36). The Christian witness receives its incarnation and force out of the calling of the people of God to be a pilgrim people giving witness to Christ our Lord in communion with the cloud of witnesses (Heb. 12:1).

Following the apostles (Acts 2:32) the church today testifies to these saving acts of God in front of the world and proclaims that Jesus Christ is Saviour and Lord of all humankind and of all creation. Such is the object of the Christian witness. Through proclamation and bearing witness, Christians are making known the saving lordship of Christ, so that the one in whom God wills to achieve this salvation may be "believed in the world" (I Tim. 3:16), so that people may confess "that Jesus Christ is Lord to the glory of God the Father" (Phil. 2:11).

The church as a whole is the primary subject of Christian witness. As the church is one body of many members, Christian witness is by its nature communitarian. When one of the faithful acts in individual witness this is related to the witness of the whole Christian community. Even when the witness is given by Christians in separated churches it should be witness to the same Christ and necessarily has a communitarian aspect.

Common Witness

When he prayed that all be one so the world might believe (John 17:21), Jesus made a clear connection between the unity of the church and the acceptance of the gospel. Unhappily Christians are still divided in their churches and the testimony they give to the gospel is thus weakened. There are, however, even now many signs of the initial unity that already exists among all followers of Christ and indications that it is developing in important ways. What we have in common, and the hope that is in us, enable us to be bold in proclaiming the gospel and trustful that the world will receive it. Common witness is the essential calling of the church and in an especial way it responds to the spirit of this ecumenical age in the church's life. It expresses our actual unity and increases our service to God's word, strengthening the churches both in proclaiming the gospel and in seeking for the fulness of unity.

Yet the tragedy of our divisions remains with us at the focal point of our testimony to Jesus: the holy eucharist. It is urgent that all Christians intensify their prayer for the full realization of this unity and witness.

"This fellowship in prayer, nevertheless, sharpens the pain of the churches' division at the point of eucharistic fellowship which should be the most manifest witness of the one sacrifice of Christ for the whole world" (*Common Witness and Proselytism*, 16).

Levels and Structures

Common witness happens and is needed at all levels of church life. Each has its own importance. Local churches and communities have evident occasions for common witness. They share the same cultural milieu and are challenged to give a clear testimony to Jesus Christ. Even small changes in attitudes at local level are a beginning for the renewal of the whole church. There should be always an interplay between witness on the local level and that on regional, national and world levels. It is important that the work for common witness takes place at all levels simultaneously.

Ecumenical groups with a specific vocation give common witness at a special level. These groups are often of a charismatic or monastic type. In dialogue with the churches they are free to search for new ways to express Christian life and common witness. They should be given support and account be taken of their findings where these have value. Church leaders could then recommend the new forms of common witness that have been tested by such groups and found to be of value.

The renewal or rediscovery of the life of monastic and religious communities in a number of churches has a special significance for common witness. In the first place it gives a new impetus to witness as such. The monastic aim springs from the desire to seek God, to bring enthusiasm for Jesus Christ into the daily routine, and to enable confession of him to dominate and colour a particular form of human existence. It embodies in a special way the keen desire that others, hearing his word and the message it contains, should also come to follow Christ. It does this especially through the witness of a Christian existence of a very deep and intense kind. Thus it makes the faith-inspired motivation which enlivens all the people of God stand out in bold relief.

As the communities of religious life in the different churches are discovering each other and their various traditions of life and witness across confessional separations, they have the potential for a major contribution to common witness. Their singleness of purpose along with their freedom to adapt to special tasks have already enabled them to contribute substantially to the ecumenical movement, but, so far, this is only a beginning in terms of the considerable spiritual resources which accrue to the vocation to the religious life.

Religious communities have a key role to play in spiritual ecumenism and in the prayer for unity. Their regular pattern of intercession gives them abundant opportunity of supporting spiritually the common witness of Christians and churches. Here those communities devoted to the liturgical and contemplative life can make a special contribution.

All groups, at local, regional or national level, have the responsibility of encouraging and inspiring each other so that they can provide examples of common witness to be used and promoted at the world level. It is highly desirable that the churches seek means of giving expression to common witness at a world level. Here the Joint Working Group between the Roman Catholic Church and the World Council of Churches may be able to give ideas and explore possibilities.

Ecumenical structures, at different levels, prove a normal occasion to discover, plan, and promote common witness. The specific purpose of such ecumenical structures is to encourage the churches in common witness and service.

These structures are of very diverse nature and range from national councils of churches through a whole variety of structures for ecumenical cooperation, to informal meetings of persons responsible for different aspects of the church's life. All can help to provide the consultation necessary to discover the situations that demand common witness.

These structures have a varied scope:
a) to encourage manifestations of common witness at local level;
b) to support those manifestations with the worldwide experience of Christians engaged in common witness and working to promote unity;
c) to introduce the ecumenical dimension into communities or groups which are already engaged in Christian witness in specific areas;
d) to organize national and regional events of a witnessing character.

CONSULTATIONS

"Confessing Christ Today," Cernica, Romania – June 4-8, 1974.
> *International Review of Mission (IRM)*, Vol. LXIV, No. 253, January 1975, pp. 64-94.

"Confessing Christ Through the Liturgical Life of the Church Today," Etchmiadzine, Armenia – September 16-21, 1975.
> *IRM*, Vol. LXIV, No. 256, October 1975, pp. 417-423.

"The Role and Place of the Bible in the Liturgical and Spiritual Life of the Orthodox Church," Prague, Czechoslovakia – September 12-18, 1977.
> *IRM*, Vol. LXVI, No. 264, October 1977, pp. 385-388.

Contribution to the theme: "Your Kingdom Come" (CWME, Melbourne, Australia, 1980), Paris, France – September 25-28, 1978.
> *IRM*, Vol. LXVIII, No. 270, April 1979, pp. 139-147.

"The Place of the Monastic Life Within the Witness of the Church Today," Amba Bishoy Monastery, Egypt – April 30-May 5, 1979.
> *IRM*, Vol. LXVIII, No. 272, October 1979, pp. 448-451.

"Preaching and Teaching the Christian Faith Today," Monastery of Zica, Yugoslavia – September 20-25, 1980.
> *IRM*, Vol. LXX, No. 278, April 1981, pp. 49-58.

Jesus Christ – the Life of the World, contribution by an Orthodox working group (Damascus, Syria, February 5-10, 1982) to the main theme of the Sixth Assembly of the World Council of Churches (Vancouver, Canada, July 1983), edited by Ion Bria, WCC, Geneva, 1982.

Just Development for Fullness of Life: An Orthodox Approach, Kiev, USSR, June 10-30, 1982, WCC Commission on the Churches' Participation in Development, Geneva, 1982.

Orthodox Thought, Reports of Orthodox Consultations organized by the WCC, 1975-1982, edited by Georges Tsetsis, WCC Geneva, 1983.

The Future of Orthodox Witness. Report of the CWME Orthodox Advisory Group, Hildesheim, Himmelsthür, FRG, October 29-November 3, 1984.

The Missionary Legacy of Ss Cyril and Methodius. Report of the CWME Orthodox Advisory Group, Sofia, Bulgaria, October 21-26, 1985.

IRM, Vol. LXXV, No. 298, April 1986, pp. 158-160.